Where Heaven Touches Earth

A Pathway of Prayer and
Change for Broken People

ROB GILES

WESTBOW
PRESS
A DIVISION OF THOMAS NELSON
& ZONDERVAN

Copyright © 2014 Rob Giles.

All rights reserved. No part of this book may be used or reproduced by any means, graphic, electronic, or mechanical, including photocopying, recording, taping or by any information storage retrieval system without the written permission of the publisher except in the case of brief quotations embodied in critical articles and reviews.

All prayers written by Rob Giles unless otherwise stated

Scripture taken from the King James Version of the Bible.

Scripture taken from the *Amplified Bible*, copyright © 1954, 1958, 1962, 1964, 1965, 1987 by The Lockman Foundation. Used by permission.

WestBow Press books may be ordered through booksellers or by contacting:

WestBow Press
A Division of Thomas Nelson & Zondervan
1663 Liberty Drive
Bloomington, IN 47403
www.westbowpress.com
1 (866) 928-1240

Because of the dynamic nature of the Internet, any web addresses or links contained in this book may have changed since publication and may no longer be valid. The views expressed in this work are solely those of the author and do not necessarily reflect the views of the publisher, and the publisher hereby disclaims any responsibility for them.

Any people depicted in stock imagery provided by Thinkstock are models, and such images are being used for illustrative purposes only.
Certain stock imagery © Thinkstock.

ISBN: 978-1-4908-5908-8 (sc)
ISBN: 978-1-4908-5909-5 (e)

Library of Congress Control Number: 2014956171

Printed in the United States of America.

WestBow Press rev. date: 12/16/2014

CONTENTS

Acknowledgements vii
Foreword ix
Preface xi

1. ...What's it all About? 1
2. ...My Story: Outrageous Grace 9
3. ...A Question of Repentance 20
4. ...Pray: Don't Give Up 29
5. ...Esther's Story: God of Miracles! 37
6. ...A Question of Suffering... 46
7. ...Pray: Praying For Others 53
8. ...Pray: Without Words..61
9. ...Contemplative Prayer: The Principles 71
10. ...Contemplative Prayer: The Biblical Basis 80
11. ...Contemplative Prayer: The How? 86
12. ...Contemplative Prayer: Quietude 94
13. ...A Question of Death...102
14. ...Clive and Sylvia's Story: Surprised by
    Peace and Love 108
15. ...A Question of Grief 116
16. ...A Question of Depression 128
17. ...A Question of Pain...134
18. ...Praying with Thanksgiving (1)............................ 141
19. ...Praying with Thanksgiving (2)............................149

20...Praying with Thanksgiving (3)............................156
21...A Question of Abuse..............................162
22...Deborah's Story: Hope, Deliverance and
       Forgiveness 170
23...A Question of Resentment 183
24...Praying with Forgiveness......................................188
25...Acceptance: The Pathway to Peace 197

References...203
Books for Further Reading..207

ACKNOWLEDGEMENTS

First and foremost I'd like to thank God, for taking me on a journey of prayer through some of life's difficulties, to lead me to a place of quiet and rest; without which this work would not have been possible.

Thanks must be given to both Sam and Indu, for allowing me the honour of writing their story. I join with them and both families in thanking God for the power of healing in the name of Jesus, and for the beautiful, bonny child, Esther has become.

Thanks also must be given to Clive and Sylvia for allowing me into their personal memories and tragic loss. Thanks be to God for the measure of healing and comfort that Jesus brings to broken hearts. I feel greatly honoured to have written their story.

Thanks to the lovely lady who has allowed me to change her name to 'Deborah'. Many thanks for sharing with me some of the horrors and dark secrets of her life. I feel greatly honoured to have been afforded the privilege of writing her story and seeing the amazing grace of God at work in her life bringing healing through forgiveness.

I would like to thank David Johnson and the

Reverend David MacPherson for writing the Foreword and Preface respectively.

Thanks to David Johnson for the amazing dedication and commitment he has shown with regard to this project. For the many hours he has spent in checking the script, for the hours we have worked together and for the input and many valuable suggestions he has made along the way (not forgetting the many cups of tea).

Thanks to the Reverend David MacPherson, a practicing psychologist, for working with me through some of my own personal issues. I am grateful that he so graciously allowed me to impose upon him to transform his endorsement into a 'short' Preface. Short being the operative word, as he said in his own words, "Psychologists say what they have to say in as few words as possible." Thanks, David.

Many thanks to Eileen Mohr for reading through the manuscript and spotting several items David J. and I had missed. Thanks to Anita Tollerton a Funeral Celebrant for her comments and much needed feedback.

Thanks to Dr Roger Bretherton and Mary Noott who have read through the manuscript and offered me such wonderful endorsements.

I'd like to thank Pastor Jill Berry for printing off the many hard copies of the manuscript that were so valuable in the process of editing and gaining much needed feedback.

Last but not least I'd like to thank WestBow Press for the way in which they have dealt with this project. Thanks to all the personnel who have worked with me, for their kindness, courtesy and support in guiding me through the publishing process.

Rob Giles 2014.

FOREWORD

It has been my privilege and pleasure to work with Rob on the production of this book. At the outset I must stress that my role in the partnership is very much a subsidiary one. Rob writes in a free, engaging and inimitable style – quite definitely 'all his own work' – and re-tells people's own true stories beautifully and poignantly. You, dear reader, will be captivated by them. I have been merely the pedant sitting at Rob's right hand when we proof-read together and, I suspect, driving him to distraction with my pepperpot of commas, colons (full and semi) and ellipses ready to sprinkle on his text at a moment's notice. I have to record that Rob is consistently gracious on those odd occasions when I suggest we might unpack a little bit of the text, test the logic and possibly re-phrase.

We have great sessions together fuelled by exceedingly strong tea and a banter borne out of our shared 'Black Country' roots (The 'Black Country' is an industrial region borne out of the Industrial Revolution in Georgian and Victorian England). Rob and I have both valued our companionship at these times. The more we worked on the book together, the more I became convinced that Rob's writing style was an invitation to readers to draw up a chair with him (by a log fire, if that's not too fanciful) and share in his and other people's stories, to share in his love of the Scriptures and to be in fellowship with him in prayer. Prayer is the breath of the Christian and Rob amply demonstrates this at the conclusion of each chapter.

This book was never intended to be a deep theological work but, in Rob's words, simply a collection of studies which give glimpses of heaven touching earth. Having said that, there are challenges on almost every page for the believer (and non-believer) expressed in Rob's straightforward language (and occasional 'Black Country' vernacular!) as much from Rob's heart as from his head.

At risk of repetition, the privilege for me has been the invitation to share at close quarters Rob's heart; the pleasure has been our tussling with the text (and drinking the odd mug of tea – typically British!).

I commend this book to you. Draw up a chair, make yourself comfortable and in your mind's eye, follow Rob's pathway of prayer. It could be life-changing.

David Johnson, Editor, 2014

PREFACE

Of the many books I have read on prayer in the past thirty plus years Rob's book is the best. It's full of down to earth no nonsense advice and will appeal both to Christian and Seeker alike.

Throughout the book Rob consistently makes the point that the Christian is not immune from normal human reactions to life's tragedies. So often Christians seem to deny the reality of their human frailty and think that somehow they should rise above reactions such as grief, depression, anger and anxiety. But Rob shows very clearly that this is not the case, and that God is with us in all the nasty parts of life as well as the good bits.

I first met Rob a few months ago when he was referred to me for counselling on some outstanding issues. We dealt with some residual problems arising from his past using an EMDR (Eye Movement De-sensitisation and Re-processing) protocol. EMDR is recognised, in the UK, by NICE (The National Institute of Clinical and Care Excellence) as an effective treatment in Post-Traumatic Stress Disorder. For those readers outside the UK, NICE is a government body set up to assess the efficacy and cost – effectiveness of all medical and psychological interventions. In Rob's case EDMR has proved to be very effective.

During the course of our discussions it became apparent that we were both Christians and during some of our consultations we spent time discussing the Christian Life. It was during these discussions that Rob mentioned that he'd written a book on prayer and kindly gave me a copy of the manuscript. I have always had an interest in contemplative prayer and have read many books on the subject. However, it seemed to me that in many of those books the authors were seeking salvation through contemplation. In Rob's book there is the acknowledgement that salvation comes through faith in Jesus Christ and that contemplative prayer is a means of deepening our relationship with God. His book is full of sound common sense. For example, how do you begin contemplative prayer? Well, you begin by turning up, to use Rob's words. To make time available just to be with God, not to ask for anything, not to intercede, but to simply be in God's presence. Being still and quiet is now recognised in psychology as an effective way of reducing stress and anxiety.

Modern psychology also touches on repentance, the biblical meaning of which is to have a change of heart and mind, followed by a change in behaviour. Changing beliefs and attitudes towards ourselves, others and life in general is a fundamental part of psychological therapies. But Jesus knew that, 2000 years ago!

Rob's book is not for the Christians who think they

have all the answers – it is for the words of Jesus "Come unto me all you who are heavy laden… and you will find rest for your souls." I pray that those who read this book will find rest for their souls and a new direction for their lives.

The Rev David MacPherson,
Cognitive behavioural Psychotherapist 2014

1

What's it all About?

"For you see your calling, brethren, that not many wise according to the flesh, not many mighty, not many noble, are called. But God has chosen the foolish things of the world to put to shame the wise, and God has chosen the weak things of the world to put to shame the things that are mighty; and the base things of the world and the things which are despised God has chosen, and the things which are not, to bring to nothing the things that are, that no flesh should glory in His presence." (1 Corinthians 1:26-29)

'Where Heaven Touches Earth'; what is meant by such a title?

Where heaven touches earth is simply the place (be it literal, physical, psychological or spiritual) where God breaks into our *personal* world to effect change: to bring light where there is darkness, faith where there is unbelief, hope where there is despair, joy where there is sorrow and forgiveness where there is hurt. This is what is meant by the title – 'Where Heaven Touches

Earth'. It is where God touches *you* and *me* where we are... in our corner.

I have written this book with broken, damaged and hurting people in mind, people who have experienced some of the harsher realities of life, hence the sub-title: 'A Pathway of Prayer and Change for Broken People'. Now I say 'change' to denote simple positive changes you and I can make for the better, *thought changes* and *behavioural changes* from bad to good, wrong to right and from sinful to pleasing God.

I have in mind those who may be having difficulty in coming to terms with the death of a loved one. For a while all of the immediate family will suffer together as one by one they come to terms with that loved one's death. If, for some reason or another, one person finds that process too difficult it may be there is no alternative but to suffer alone. Feeling pressured by well-meaning family to come to terms with that death is not a nice place to be. One cannot talk to anyone about it for fear of criticism. Consequently they will feel condemned and isolated. My questions are these:

"Can such broken-hearted people find God in the midst of their heartache and loss?" "Is there a gracious and loving God who is willing to draw alongside and step into their world and bring comfort?"

* * *

I also have in mind those who suffer from depression. Depression is a subject that doesn't seem to be talked about too often in Christian circles. There appears to be some sort of stigma attached to mental illness. The stigma is not in depression per se but lies in people's perception of it. Depression is a real illness which can become very debilitating. Sufferers are often urged to pull themselves together but, of course, they cannot. People say, "You shouldn't be down. You should be happy and grateful for all the good God has done for you." Consequently sufferers of depression can feel isolated because no one seems to understand. The danger for them is to suffer alone by hiding themselves away. Many who are depressed carry with them a feeling of low self-esteem and a certain amount of self-condemnation anyway, so to make them feel condemned will only add to their depression.

I ask these questions: "Can a person with mental illness find God in the midst of depression?" "Is there a gracious and loving God who is willing to draw alongside to bring comfort and gently lead them to recovery?"

* * *

I also have in mind those who struggle with alcohol and drug abuse. Now this is a tricky one, for such a statement can be easily misconstrued. Alcohol and drug abuse are sins against God and they are sins against our own bodies and minds. You may say to me, "That's a strong statement." Allow me to explain.

There is a huge difference between an alcoholic, and an alcoholic struggling with alcohol. You may say to me, 'What on earth are you talking about?' 'You're out of your mind' or 'You're talking in riddles.'

While the alcoholic or drug addict is in what is called 'denial', they cannot be helped. Denial is the place where the alcoholic or addict feels they do not have a problem or if they do, they think they are in control. The alcoholic or addict thinks and declares publicly, 'I don't have a problem.' They deny having a problem, therefore they cannot be helped.

During the period of denial, which may last a lifetime, the 'ranting and raving' or violence, the lies, the stealing and deception can be so unbearably horrible for family and loved ones. The family struggles with the devastating effects of alcoholism or addiction while the alcoholic or addict is completely oblivious. Alcoholism not only affects the user but it can destroy families. I know this to be true from my own personal experience.

This is the awful sin of alcoholism and addiction.

There may be no alternative for parents than to put them out, if they live at home. You cannot keep bailing them out. The family may even have to involve the police. The father in the prodigal son story let his son go, and when he was in dire straits the father did not seek him out. It's what we call these days 'tough love' but, there may be no other alternative. There is no talking sense to an alcoholic or drug addict in denial. They have to find out the hard way and hit rock-bottom before they will begin to seek help, just as the prodigal did.

There may come a point in the lives of some alcoholics and drug addicts when they do hit rock-bottom, where they become consumed by guilt, shame and condemnation. To the onlooker their actions may still appear to be the same, but inside the heart and mind of the addict or alcoholic, guilt, shame and condemnation, become soul-destroying. They long to get free... but they cannot. This is where I would say they are *struggling* with addiction. But I wouldn't say an alcoholic or drug addict is *struggling* with addiction until this stage is reached.

The broken and shattered soul craves unconditional love but cannot find it. The overwhelming sense of guilt of *sinning deliberately* (because that is how it can feel) may become impossible to live with for the alcoholic or addict. So I ask the questions:

"Where then does this tortured soul go?" "To whom do they turn?" "Is there a way out?" "Is there a way back to God?" "Is there a loving, gracious God who is willing to draw near, restore, forgive, bring healing and set free the tortured mind and bring deliverance from addiction?"

* * *

I also have in mind people who have been sexually abused or raped. I'm sure all of us are aware that sexual abuse and rape are heinous crimes causing untold damage to the victims. They are both sins against God and crimes against humanity. Tragically, sexual abuse and rape are real and very prevalent in today's world.

Victims of abuse and rape do not have a voice because abuse and rape are taboo subjects, and as such, they're not topics to be freely talked about. And they are certainly not subjects to be talked about in a church setting. But they should be. There are a large number of women and men (surprisingly) who have been abused (as children) or raped… and many of them are in our congregations. The sad thing is, the majority still struggle with the consequences. They may spend the remainder of their lives haunted by what has taken place simply because they cannot find a way to resolve their issues.

If or when the victim of rape or abuse gets a voice, it appears there is no reason other than to relive the event, to be humiliated and to feel violated all over again both mentally and emotionally. So I ask the questions:

"How then do they find a way through their heartache, pain and violation?" Or even "Is there a way through?" "Is there a loving and gracious God who is able to draw near, to share their pain and to heal their bleeding heart?" "Is there a way to peace?"

* * *

I also have in mind people who have been hurt by someone or some event; as a result, they carry a load of bitterness and resentment in their hearts. The resentment eats them up. They may feel, in their heart of hearts, that it is wrong to be resentful but they cannot stop, nor can they find a way of resolving the gnawing issues that caused it. So I ask:

"Is there a way out?" "Is there a loving God who is able to draw alongside, forgive, and bring healing?"

This book is written for such people. It is also written for anyone who feels marginalized or condemned. It is written for anyone who feels that life is simply too much. And it is written for anyone struggling with their sin or with the consequences of it.

This book is not a theological or academic treatise nor is it meant to be. It is simply a collection of studies, a record of one broken soul speaking to another broken soul. It is therefore, friendly, simple, gentle, peaceful and intentionally conversational. It often states the obvious but sometimes when we are hurting, aspects of the obvious are what we fail to see.

I don't offer anything new in terms of biblical

revelation. I take the *simple*, childlike, tried and tested methods of prayer and I use them to assist the reader to draw near to God. As you will see from my own story, simple prayer was the main *tool* God used to set me free from the sin of alcoholism.

I combine my *simple* approach to prayer with the *simple*, tried and tested advice offered through psychotherapy, support groups and counselling. By so doing, I'm not offering an alternative way, but an additional way of working through and challenging the difficulties that have the potential to ruin our lives.

There are three personal stories in this work besides my own. One is the disturbing story of a woman who was systematically abused by her step father when she was a child. I have changed her name for obvious reasons.

Each story is a powerful example of *Heaven Touching Earth*. The reason for their inclusion is that testimonies encourage. They challenge, inspire, build faith and they give glory to God. Testimonies are like windows shedding light and providing challenging and life-changing illustrations. These stories introduce difficult topics by way of personal and intimate experience. In addition, they provide me with the means of exploring such difficult topics as suffering, death, grief, depression, pain, abuse, bitterness and resentment on a deeper level.

You may feel like asking several questions at this point: "Can I really get through such dark experiences, feelings and emotions?" "Can I really find God in the midst of my troubles and woes?" "Can I come through to a place of *peace*?" or "Can I have the assurance that God is near, even though *my* world is falling apart?"

Let me allay your doubts and fears. There *is* a way out and there *is* a way through, with God at our side. We may not get through our difficulties in the way we would like but we can certainly come to a place where we dare to believe, "I *can* get through this!"

We can: come to a place where we find the courage to face our past, where we may deal with our sins, debilitating anxieties, griefs and resentments. We can: come to a place where we have the conviction that God's grace *is* sufficient for our future even though we may have messed up thoroughly and violated His laws.

We can: come to a place of wholeness and peace with a thankful heart - where God breaks into our personal world to effect change: to bring light where there is darkness, faith where there is unbelief, hope where there is despair, joy where there is sorrow and forgiveness where there is hurt - to a place 'Where Heaven Touches Earth' - your *earth* and my *earth*.

Will you allow 'Heaven' to touch you where you are?

Dear Lord, as I choose to read on, I pray that You will be with me. Grant me ears to hear Your message and a heart to obey it. Help me, O God, to come to the place where I may bring my issues to You. Give me the grace to be able to face them and lead me to a place of peace and rest in the name of Jesus Christ of Nazareth. Amen. (Prayer written by Rob Giles 2014)

2

My Story: Outrageous Grace

"Save me, O God! For the waters have come up to my neck. I sink in deep mire, where there is no standing. (Psalm 69:1&2) "...But when he was still a great way off, his father saw him and had compassion, and ran and fell on his neck and kissed him. And the son said to him, 'Father, I have sinned against heaven and in your sight, and am no longer worthy to be called your son'. But the father said to his servants, 'Bring out the best robe and put it on him, and put a ring on his hand and sandals on his feet. And bring the fatted calf here and kill it, and let us eat and be merry; for this my son was dead and is alive again; he was lost and is found.' (Luke 15:20-24) "...I did not come to call the righteous, but sinners, to repentance." (Matthew Psalm 9:13)

I graduated from Bible College in '96. For me, it was late in life; I was forty six. My application for ordination was accepted on the grounds of the mission work I was involved in. I was part of a team taking aid from the UK to Bosnian refugee camps in war-torn Croatia. Our main contact was a loving Croatian pastor who made it his job to reach out to Bosnian refugees in private accommodation by taking them food parcels. These people were outside the refugee camps and largely forgotten. It was a wonderful privilege to go with him in his little car to visit a family, take a gift box and place it in their hands. It was a very humbling experience. I made several trips to Croatia and enjoyed the work immensely.

Later, my wife and I travelled to Romania. We visited the street kids who lived in the sewers beneath a large city. We played soccer with the kids on a large car park near to a railway station. We fed them sandwiches and gave them drinks of orange squash. The intention was to build friendships so as to encourage them off the streets to be cared for in a Christian-run home and be educated to a level whereby they could be accepted and integrated back into mainstream education. In my mind, looking back, this was an awesome period of my life.

While holding down a secular job, I became the pastor of a small church. They couldn't afford to pay me and so I supported myself and family through my secular job. I loved the pastoral work. I loved delving into the Scriptures and taking Bible studies but I disliked my secular job.

I was a qualified engineer. The job I was in was highly skilled and highly pressurised and the pressure slowly ground me down. When I resigned as pastor because of family commitments, I'll be honest, it broke my heart.

I encouraged myself by saying, 'God has something more for me to do…' but it didn't happen. Every avenue

I pursued was closed to me. I became depressed as my world slowly fell apart. I eventually broke down mentally and emotionally. I turned to alcohol in a vain attempt to get by from day to day. At first, alcohol was pleasant but after a while it became a nightmare, torturing my mind. Depression and alcohol do not mix!

Once I had opened up my life to the sin of alcoholism, sin came in like a flood. I became addicted to alcohol. You know you are addicted when you cannot live without it. You know you are addicted when you want to stop drinking, but you can't.

I was tortured by this, my sin. The weight of it and the sense of condemnation caused me extreme mental and emotional anguish.

I felt the Bible condemned me. I could not get over, around or work through, certain verses of Scripture.

I felt the Church condemned me. I couldn't work through certain theological issues and Christian doctrines even though I repented of my sin on a daily basis. I went forward in Church meetings but found no respite or release.

I felt Christians condemned me. They told me what I was doing was sin. 'Tell me something I don't know,' I would say. What they were saying was perfectly true, of course, but I didn't need anyone to tell me it was a sin, I knew it. I needed someone to show me a way out!

My own heart condemned me. I couldn't get over, around or work through my sin. At one point I prayed on an hourly basis. I confessed my sin and asked God to forgive me and I repented as best I knew how. I continued to go forward in Church meetings looking for prayer and deliverance. But nothing seemed to work. The critical question for me at that time was, 'Is there a way back for me?' I doubted there was.

Night after night I lay on my bed and cried myself to sleep. I called out to God for help and deliverance. I had awful, horrifying visions, dreams and nightmares. I say visions because I had them during the daytime; I couldn't switch them off. I feared insanity.

I was filled with remorse. Being unable to find a way out took me to the brink of suicide. One by one my sins began to stack up. I prayed to die. I didn't really want to die but the life I had seemed unbearable.

Here I pause for a moment.

Remorse is a powerful emotion. When I look back, I recognise that *remorse* was there in my depression and it was there in the later stages of my addiction. Judas Iscariot was remorseful and went out and hanged himself (Matthew 27:3-5). Depression and remorse can become all consuming. Add alcohol or drugs to that mix and the result can be fatal. If not resolved, remorse can become engulfed in despair and hopelessness, which in turn can lead to suicidal thoughts, suicidal attempts or even suicide itself.

For almost four years this destructive storm raged.

Slowly it became clear to me that I was actually in bondage. Although not physically bound with ropes or chains, but I was mentally and emotionally. Looking back I've often thought, 'How ever did I manage to survive?'

One night everything changed, suddenly and dramatically. I don't know why and I don't know how. I certainly didn't deserve what took place, nor did I do anything to warrant it. What did take place was beyond anything I could ever have dreamt of or imagined.

I had gone to bed early. It must have been around 9.30 p.m. I lay on my bed, as usual, crying myself to sleep. Suddenly, Jesus came and stood at the foot of my bed. I was terrified. I genuinely thought He'd come to take me.

My whole life seemed to flash before me in a moment of time… (It is true what they say!) It was as though I was stripped naked from the inside out. There was nowhere to run and there was nowhere to hide. I was completely in His hands. This was my reality; there was no time for excuses. I thought, *'If He mentions my sin, I will certainly die'*.

But He didn't, He said nothing.

I was confused.

Instead He came and sat on my bed and embraced me and wept on my shoulder. I fell apart inside and cried violently, rivers of tears. I thought, *'You shouldn't be doing this. This is no way for the Son of God to behave'*. My body convulsed with the power of my crying. Through my sobs I asked, 'Why are you doing this.' He replied 'It is grace, Rob. It's simply grace.' Then He lay by my side and I fell asleep in His arms.

Was this for real?

Was it an apparition or a dream?

I cannot say. But it changed my life. That night I slept peacefully for the first time in five years.

At this point you may be wondering, 'Why?' 'Why would Jesus come to a wretch like me? There are far better people out there than me and many who are much more deserving!'

I've asked myself the same questions, time and time again. All I can possibly do is just accept His 'outrageous grace', accept the love He gave and accept the message He brought to me. It serves no purpose at all in my trying to work it out.

The following evening I went to bed early and lay on my bed propped up with pillows to pray. To my astonishment Jesus came again and stood at the bottom of my bed.

'Your mind is shot,' He said to me. I marvelled at His choice of words, but what He said confirmed to me what I already suspected; my mind was indeed damaged. 'But I have come to change your way of thinking,' He said. 'Don't be afraid, just trust me. We will work through this together.' When He said 'trust Me' I somehow felt I could.

'Do you want the easy way or the hard way?' He asked. I thought, *Oh no, don't give me a choice.* So I answered, 'You choose.'

'I'll take you the hard way. You'll have to fight for everything you get. But I will take you the easy way into My presence. Just one thought and you will be with Me. I'm not asking you to do anything difficult, just turn up'

Quite what He meant by that, I was unsure. I somehow sensed there would be no instant deliverance from alcohol. But by the same token I also sensed He would do something dramatic through prayer; He did.

During the next three months He came to me almost every day. Sometimes He would come in the evening and at other times He would come in the small hours of the morning. He taught me to change my thinking by setting my mind upon Him. He also taught me a ridiculously simple means of prayer, which opened up to me the presence of God in a new way. At that particular point in time I didn't know what this simple way of prayer was called. But around two weeks later, I came into contact with a book entitled *Spiritual Torrents* by Jeanne Guyon. After reading the book I became aware that the way I was praying was in fact contemplative prayer.

Many aspects of my life were transformed in an instant. My attitude changed and my depression lifted but I still wasn't totally free from alcohol. I used contemplative prayer for around one hour each morning and then as often as I could throughout my day I would reflect on Jesus; I would contemplate God. These simple processes began to change my thinking. The changes which took place in a relatively short space of time were astonishing.

One morning when He came to me in the small hours, He opened up to me Romans 7:17–25. I was shocked that twice in the passage Paul said *"But now, it is no longer I who do it, but sin that dwells in me." (verse 17)* and *"Now if I do what I will not to do, it is no longer I who do it, but sin that dwells in me." (verse 20)* Often when something is repeated in the Scriptures it is something to take note of.

I have to admit, these verses were very hard to swallow. Their message cut across what I had been taught as a Christian. It seemed as though the Lord was offering me an excuse! That frightened me. In fact, those two verses terrified me.

The Lord continued with the Scripture, *"I find then a law, that evil is present with me, the one who wills to do good." (verse 21)* The Lord said to me, 'Do you 'will' to stop drinking?' 'Yes' I replied. The Scripture continued, *"For I delight in the law of God according to the inward* man." *(verse 22)* 'Do you delight in the law of God in your inner man?' He asked. 'Yes I do.'

He continued once more with the Scripture. *"But I see another law in my members, warring against the law of my mind, and bringing me into captivity to the law of sin which is in my members." (verse 23)* He emphasised the law of *my mind* and linked it to the *will* to do good and to the *delight* in the law of God, showing me that the *will* and the *delight* both come from the *mind*. The law of sin and death was *warring against my mind and bringing me into captivity,* (i.e. bondage) *to the law of sin.*

Then He continued with the Scripture, *"O wretched man that I am! Who will deliver me from this body of death?" (verse 24)* This was a perfect description of how I felt at that particular moment of time in my addiction. I was trapped and I could not get free. *O wretched man that I am!* and *this body of death* were very real to me. It was as though the Apostle Paul who wrote the book of Romans was crying out to God with the same degree of pain and with the same degree of helplessness that I felt.

Then the Lord Jesus continued once more with the Scripture, *"I thank God - through Jesus Christ our Lord! So then with the mind I myself serve the law of God, but with the flesh the law of sin." (verse 25)* He emphasised *the mind*. I now felt that I had the power to serve the law of God, (the Word of God… the Scriptures) with my mind because of what Christ had done on the cross. I now had the power to *think* on the Word, to *think* on God, to *think* on righteousness, to *think* on good…

It seemed awesome to me at that moment in time. I realised that my mind needed to be renewed. I became aware that I had a part to play in that renewal process.

The renewal of my mind was certainly something worth fighting for. The mind is a powerful tool and a powerful gift from God; I should use it. I began to understand that with my mind I *willed* to do that which was right, i.e. stop drinking. With my mind I *delighted* in the Lord and I *delighted* in His word. This was the beginning of the freedom process. I held in my mind the *will* to stop drinking. I embraced, fostered, and courted... whatever you want to call it, the *delight* in God and the *delight* in God's word.

With my *mind* I began to serve God. I began to focus my mind upon Jesus Christ as much as I could. I found that contemplative prayer was a great tool and a great help in that process. I tried to think on God as often as I could throughout the day as I worked. I also tried to fill my mind with the Scriptures as much as I could.

You might say to me, "Why say *try*? You either do it or you don't." Good point. But it doesn't quite work that way. When you are working or attempting to work in cooperation with God, such as in renewal of the mind, the task can seem enormous but the result is of eternal value. How can you say you've achieved it perfectly? You can't. *Try* or *attempt* is the most a fallible human being can achieve. Only God can do it perfectly. Our part is simply to cooperate with Him and then to trust Him for the outcome.

Often I repeated a verse of Scripture over and over in my mind while I worked. Sometimes I would pray for someone else. To my astonishment my drinking diminished drastically, but I still wasn't completely free. For me, to be completely free, was to stop drinking all together and stay that way. It was a long hard process.

In fact, it took thirteen months in total, from the first visitation until I took my last drink. I remember that day well.

I'd finished work early around 2.00 in the afternoon and called at a bar on my way home. At that period of my life I would drink just one pint, possibly Guinness, but never more than two, then I'd go home. On this occasion I had drunk probably three quarters of my pint when suddenly I became aware that I was ogling the barmaid. There were no outward sexual gestures from me nor were there any sexual innuendo, it was purely an inner thought that I suddenly became aware of. But even our thoughts can be sinful. I thought to myself "I don't want this rubbish any more." So I drank up and walked out. As I opened the door and crossed the threshold to exit the building, I literally felt something break inside of me and something lifted off me. I knew I was free. From that day, November 17th 2004, 2.30 in the afternoon, to this, alcohol has not passed my lips.

Although I knew that I was free I did not stop my way of prayer. I continued with it. 'Let's go further with God' was my thinking. Contemplative prayer had opened up for me a reality of God beyond my wildest dreams.

This book is an offering of what the Lord has taught me. It is my offering, from one simple, broken soul to another. It is all about the quiet way of contemplation and of how it may be used to assist in the renewal of the mind. It is about making simple changes in our thinking, which in turn, will bring about simple changes in our lives in cooperation with the Holy Spirit. It is all about simple changes you and I can make for the better. In other words it's much the same as repentance. For true repentance, as we shall see, is a change of mind or a change of purpose leading to a change of direction or a change of behaviour.

> *"Heavenly Father, I thank you for the 'Outrageous Grace' you have poured out upon each one of us through the work of your Son, the Lord Jesus Christ, on the cross. Enlighten our minds through the Holy Spirit and teach us the way of freedom. Teach us to use our minds. Teach us not to go mindless from one event to another but to think carefully on what we are doing. Help us to make the appropriate changes in cooperation with Your Word through the Holy Spirit. I ask this in the name of Jesus. Amen. (Prayer written by Rob Giles 2014)*

3

A Question of Repentance

"...And saying, repent (think differently; change your mind, regretting your sins and changing your conduct) for the kingdom of heaven is at hand. (Matthew 3:2. The Amplified Bible). "John the Baptist appeared in the wilderness (desert), preaching a baptism [obligating] repentance (a change of one's mind for the better, heartily amending one's ways, with abhorrence of his past sins) in order to obtain forgiveness of and release from sins." (Mark 1:4. The Amplified Bible). "Jesus came into Galilee, preaching the good news (Gospel) of the kingdom of God), and saying, 'The [appointed period of] time is fulfilled (completed), and the kingdom of God is at hand; repent (have a change of mind which issues in regret for past sins and in change of conduct for the better) and believe (trust in, rely on, and adhere to) the good news (the Gospel). (Mark 1:14b&15. The Amplified Bible)

Repentance, according to the Collins English Dictionary & Thesaurus is, *"To show remorse (for) be contrite (about) show penitence (for)"* [1]

There is a verse of Scripture that says; *"If we confess ours sins, He is faithful and just to forgive us our sins and to cleanse us from all unrighteousness."* (1 John 1:9)

As Christians it should be our practice to confess our sins to God in prayer, whenever we are conscious that we have sinned. In addition, we should ask God to forgive us, as taught in the Lord's Prayer. *"And forgive us our sins, for we also forgive everyone who is indebted to us."* (Luke 11: 4) Our practice then should be: confess our sins to God, tell God we are sorry and ask Him to forgive us.

Confession is personal and confession is crucial.

Confession means that we take ownership of what we have done. When we confess we are in fact, 'owning-up' to our sins. "I have done this" or "I have done that." Should there be a third party involved then we must cease apportioning blame to the other person, by saying, "It was their fault" or "they made me do it'. No, we take ownership of what we have done, personally - no excuses.

Confession is crucial in our day to day walk with God. Years ago, the imperative was, 'keep short accounts with God regarding sin'. Today, in our fast moving, high-tech world we seem to have lost sight of that directive. Confession, being sorry and asking God to forgive us - is the right and proper way forward for the Christian.

Confession is often confused with repentance by the church, but they are different. The word 'repent', according to dictionary definition, lets us off the hook somewhat, for while it reveals remorse, contrition and penitence, it doesn't emphasise 'stop doing it', 'turn away from it' or 'amending your ways'. Repentance, from the original, New Testament Greek perspective, is much more than confession. It is much more than being sorry and asking God to forgive you.

The New Testament Greek word is *metanoeo*. Phonetically pronounced met-an-o-eh'-o, it means:

"To change one's mind or purpose" [2]

In New Testament times, *metanoeo* was an everyday word which simply meant to change one's mind, adopt another view or to change one's feelings, as in; 'I was going to do this, now I'm going to do that', 'I believed this, now I believe that' or 'I felt like thumping him but I changed my mind'. There might be an element of regret attached to the word *metanoeo* depending on the occasion or the context in which it is used. For instance, if the change of mind was brought about by a feeling that the original view was perceived to be foolish or improper there might be an element of regret. There might also be a change in conduct inferred in *metanoeo*, if the original course of action was thought to be evil or sinful.

The Amplified Bible, kindly gives us, several definitions of the word *metanoeo* taken from the very best New Testament Greek Lexicons. Firstly, *(think differently: change your mind, regretting your sins and changing your conduct) Matthew 3:2*. Secondly, *(a change of one's mind for the better, heartily amending one's ways, with abhorrence of his past sins) Mark 1:4*. Thirdly, *(have a change of mind which issues in regret for past sins and in change of conduct for the better) Mark 1:14b&15*.

If you look up Mark 1:4 in The Amplified Bible, for instance, you will notice that the definition in brackets is numbered to a footnote directing the reader to the source of the definition, i.e. *"Joseph Thayer. A Greek - English Lexicon of the New Testament."* [3]

From the above definitions of *metanoeo*, found in The Amplified Bible, we discover that repentance has three basic ingredients: a change of mind, regret and a change of conduct.

Firstly, change your mind. All of our actions stem from our thoughts. *"For as he thinks in his heart, so is he." (Proverbs 23:7)* Fill your mind with garbage, filth or evil then garbage, filth and evil will pervade your life. Fill your mind with thoughts of God, and of good things then you will more than likely do good things. The Apostle Paul said:

"Whatever things are true, whatever things are noble, whatever things are just, whatever things are pure, whatever things are lovely, whatever things are of good report, if there is any virtue and if there is anything praiseworthy meditate on these things." (Philippians 4:8)

And again:

"For those who live according to the flesh set their minds on the things of the flesh, but those who live according to the Spirit, the things of the Spirit. For to be carnally minded is death, but to be spiritually minded is life and peace." (Romans 8:5)

Change the way you think... change what you think... and you will more than likely change the way you behave.

Secondly, regret. Regretting your sin is being sorry for what you have done and wishing you hadn't done it. Abhorrence takes it one step further. It means that you find your personal sin repugnant or loathsome. This is far more than merely being sorry. Abhorrence of sin is something that's not often taught in Christian circles these days - but it should be. It may make us more serious about following after righteousness. Regret, then, is wishing you hadn't done it.

Thirdly, change your conduct or change your behaviour, heartily amending your ways for the better (Mark 1:4). This is a massive step beyond confession and merely saying sorry. Let's be clear, that's not dismissing their importance. Confession and being sorry have their rightful place in Christian behaviour but they do not constitute repentance. Many are the Christians who have confessed their sins, said sorry and asked God to forgive them, then they have stepped outside and committed the same sin all over again. My analysis may be overly simplistic but this behaviour is not repentance.

Repentance means you stop doing what you're doing and you replace it with something else. Listen to the words of Paul, *"Let him who stole, steal no longer, but rather let him labor, working with his hands what is good, that he may have something to give him who has need." (Ephesians 4:28)* Stop doing it and replace it with something else or as John the Baptist said, *"Therefore bear fruits worthy of repentance." (Matthew 3:8)* In other words 'bear fruit worthy of a change of mind'. If you have changed your mind make sure your actions prove it. So I ask the question, "If you were going to 'thump Jimmy' but you changed your mind (you repented), would you then go ahead and thump him?"

My journey in walking free from the sin of alcoholism has taught me one thing - simple yet profound - repenting of alcohol is not complete until you stop drinking and you remain abstinent. If you cannot stop then it is not repentance.

True repentance, is to change your mind, regret what you have done and set about amending your ways. Stop what you are doing 'wrong' and replace it with something 'right'. Stop what you are doing 'bad' and replace it with something 'good'. Stop what you are doing 'sinful' and replace it with something 'pleasing to God'.

If *metanoeo* is a change of mind, then we should be able to *'metanoeo'* before we contemplate sinning. In other words we should be able to change our mind (repent) before the sin is committed.

You might say to me, "That's a freaky statement," or "You are talking in riddles". "You're out of your mind" "Surely no one can repent until after they have sinned!"

If we follow the dictionary definition of the English word repent, then to repent *after* we have sinned may be the only option. But if we follow the New Testament word *metanoeo* then it opens up to us an astonishing new option - change your mind *before* you sin and so stop yourself from sinning. I was going to 'thump Jimmy' but I changed my mind and didn't thump him.

To explain further, let's take a look at a verse of Scripture found in the epistle of James.

"But each one is tempted when he is drawn away by his own desires and enticed. Then, when the desire has conceived, it brings forth sin; and sin, when it is full-grown, brings forth death." (James 1:14)

I don't know if you are like me but I found it quite surprising to discover that the 'desires', according to this verse, come from within; they come from you and they come from me, not the devil. Shock... horror. But that is what the Scripture says. *"...each one is tempted when he is drawn away by his own desires..."*

Just stop and think about the implications of this for one moment. It means that sin is something innate. It is up to you and it's up to me, as Christians, to turn from sin and believe the Gospel. No one can do that for you. You have to make the choice yourself. Human beings are very good at apportioning blame and Christians are very good at apportioning blame to the 'devil' whether it is true or false, founded or unfounded.

The verse says, *"...drawn away by his own desires and enticed"*. Let's be clear on this. The *'enticing'* is the work of the devil but the *'desires'* are our own.

The verse continues. *"Then, when the desire has conceived, it brings forth sin."*

The word *then* is crucial to the verse, and crucial to its interpretation. The word *then* divides this verse of Scripture into two. Something is happening, *then*, something else takes place. It is what one might term 'cause and effect'. The cause: *"...each one is tempted when he is drawn away by his own desires and enticed"*. Then the effect: *"when the desire has conceived, it brings forth sin; and sin, when it is full-grown, brings forth death."*

The Christian *then* has a choice. When the temptation comes, either we go along mindlessly, without thought, and then *sin* or, when the temptation comes, we change our mind in favour of another course of action.

We do not have to wait until we have sinned before we change our minds, *metanoeo*, repent. Between the 'enticing desires' and the 'conception that brings forth sin' is the place to *metanoeo*. This is the place to change ones mind. It is what I would call overcoming temptation. The mind is an amazing piece of technology, a God-given tool, a God-given gift; we should use it.

Psalm 119:9 says, *"How shall a young man cleanse his way? By taking heed and keeping watch [on himself] according to your word [conforming his life to it]." (Psalm 119:9. The Amplified Bible).*

I notice three things from this text.

Firstly, *'by taking heed and keeping watch [on himself]'.* This means being observant and watchful. It means being 'mindful' of what we are thinking, saying or doing. Most of us live out certain areas of our life habitually and thoughtlessly. Our reactions and responses are spontaneous, quick, unmeasured, instinctive and automatic. Being 'mindful' will change that. It is what Jesus meant when He said, "Watch and pray, lest you enter into temptation." (Matthew 26:41). Watching is being 'mindful' of what we are thinking, saying and doing. But we will only achieve this type of 'watching' by slowing down inside and being thoughtful. Being quiet and still within will allow us time and space to momentarily consider or reconsider our responses.

The second thing I notice from Psalm 119:9 is the phrase *'according to your word'*. This reveals to us the importance of knowing the Scriptures. Unless we read the Word of God and get to know the Word, we will never know how God wants us to respond, think, speak or act in a given situation.

The third thing I notice from Psalm 119:9 is this: *'according to your word [conforming one's life to it]'* i.e. knowing the Word of God and putting it into practice. By so doing our lives will slowly be conformed to the Word of God. It means changing one's mind, effectuating a change of heart and transforming one's ways in favour of God's ways… which brings us neatly back to *metanoeo…* repentance.

We will never live a life conformed to the Word of

God by living thoughtlessly, habitually unmeasured and impulsive. But we will achieve it through 'watching'. We will achieve it by being mindful of what is going on around us and inside of us. And we will achieve it through being quiet and still within. This is why I believe contemplative prayer can play such an important role in our day to day Christian walk, in repentance, in prayer, in worship and in living our lives for God.

Dear Lord, I pray that You will give me ears to hear and a heart to follow You. May I be willing to heed Your call to change. Holy Spirit, draw near to me and teach me how I may be mindful of my thoughts and responses before I actually act. So that, in cooperation with You, I may walk in repentance and live out my life to honour You in all my ways. Amen. (Prayer written by Rob Giles 2014)

4

Pray: Don't Give Up

"...men always ought to pray and not lose heart" (Luke 18:1). "Is anyone among you suffering? Let him pray..." (James 5:13) "Ask, and it will be given to you; seek, and you will find; knock, and it will be opened to you. For everyone who asks receives, and he who seeks finds, and to him who knocks it will be opened." (Matthew 7:7&8)

In beginning our journey together, it is important that we draw a definite distinction between theorising on prayer and performing it in reality. All of the various teachings, concepts and theories regarding prayer are worthless unless we can take them, use them and put them into practice. There is no substitute for *actually* praying.

The appropriate Biblical response in any situation is to pray. Jesus said, *"...men always ought to pray and not lose heart" (Luke 18:1).* And more specifically, the appropriate Biblical response to adversity is to pray; *"Is anyone among you suffering? Let him pray..." (James 5:13)* We may ask, "Why pray?"

Prayer does appear to be a natural response. Most people, even if they do not believe, will offer up some sort of prayer when disaster strikes. It's something almost instinctive that is *inbuilt* into each of us. I think James must have thought similarly when he penned those words, exhorting us to pray when we suffer.

In point of fact, James is not asking us to do something difficult, go to the ends of the earth, change our philosophy or undergo therapy. He simply exhorts us to pray.

God communicates with us in many ways: through the Scriptures, via the Holy Spirit, through another person, through a sermon or sequence of events - but our only means of communication with Him is through prayer. The thought of us, mere mortals, talking directly to God is an astonishing concept. The reality - that God chooses to listen - is even more astounding! God hears our prayers! God answers prayer! Prayer changes things; we therefore, ought to pray.

We are encouraged to believe that Christ is always with us and that we are not alone. Jesus said:

"...In the world you will have tribulation; but be of good cheer, I have overcome the world." (John 16:33)

He also said:

"...and lo, I am with you always, even to the end of the age." (Matthew 28:20) and again; *"...I will never leave you nor forsake you." (Hebrews 13:5)*

The above verses are written to give us the assurance that we are not alone. They may also become a living reality the more we pray and the more we put our trust in God.

If I were to say, "Prayer is vast and boundless", you might respond by saying, "That's a strong statement!"

In my view prayer is vast because there is such a *vast* array of different types of prayer and different ways of praying.

Prayer is boundless because we are praying to a *boundless* God and there is nothing that cannot be achieved through prayer. Lives have been changed by it, situations have been changed by it and circumstances have been changed by it. Neighbourhoods have been changed by it and even whole nations have been changed by it.

Prayer is boundless because no one can put prayer *in a box* by saying "this is the only way it's done" or "prayer only works this way". The moment we put parameters on prayer, it becomes less effective and is therefore in danger of failure.

Prayer is boundless because prayer is far more than mere words. First and foremost, prayer is effectual through the voice from the heart. But it is also effectual through the mind and through the will; it touches our senses, emotions and feelings and it flows through our tears, sighs and agonising groans.

Prayer is boundless because it can lead individuals to a far *richer* and more *fulfilled* life. I'm not talking particularly about the *riches* of this world - money, wealth, fame etc. I'm talking about the *riches* of the heart made manifest in love, joy, peace, kindness and generosity. I'm talking about *fulfilment* in terms of contentment: contentment with one's self, contentment with God and contentment with the circumstances in which we find ourselves. This, I believe, is true fulfilment.

Prayer is effective and prayer is fruitful. It is *effective* because as we pray we are taking steps in obedience to the Word of God: *"...men always ought to pray and not lose heart" (Luke 18:1).* Prayer is *fruitful* because the more we do it; the more likely we are of fulfilling the Apostle Paul's extraordinary exhortation: *"pray without ceasing," (1Thessalonians 5:17).* As I see it, unceasing prayer can only be achieved through intimacy with God and will deepen our relationship with Him. In the light of these things, it is not surprising that James says these words; *"Is anyone among you suffering? Let him pray..." (James 5:13)*

The benefits gained through prayer far outweigh whatever we may lose, or appear to lose, in any period of trial or difficulty. Paul said:

"For I consider the sufferings of this present time are not worthy to be compared with the glory which shall be revealed in us." (Romans 8:18)

Trusting God through thick and thin is right at the heart of the Christian faith, and sharing our burdens with Him in prayer, is one way of expressing that trust. If we are to find God in the midst of our troubles, then surely we must be giving ourselves to prayer!

The Apostle Paul in his letter to the Philippians encouraged his readers to pray at all times and in every situation:

"Be anxious for nothing, but in everything by prayer and supplication, with thanksgiving, let your requests be made know to God;" (Philippians 4:6).

We're not told how to pray, where to pray, when to pray, or what to pray (with the exception of the Lord's Prayer); we're merely urged to pray. One of the greatest mysteries of prayer is that there will never be a situation too difficult or too trivial to bring before God. When the Apostle said, *"in everything by prayer",* I think we can safely say he meant *everything.*

One need only take a cursory look through the book of Psalms to discover that David shared everything with God. Every feeling, every emotion, every question, every grievance; whether he was up or down, happy or sad, he laid all before the Almighty. When he failed, often miserably, he was not afraid to humble himself and confess all to the Lord. *Psalm 51* is a classic example and a great lesson for us all to learn. We would do well to follow David's example by sharing everything with God in prayer.

We in the West have sometimes been guilty of making prayer far too complicated. That which should be second nature to us has somehow become far too difficult. Whilst prayer is indeed *vast and boundless*, it need not be complex.

Prayer is simple - and yet profound, unsophisticated - yet powerful, unpretentious - yet all prevailing!

There will be times, of course, when our prayers will appear to rise no higher than the ceiling and God himself will seem a million miles away. There will be times when we will feel we cannot pray, don't know how to pray, don't want to pray, or even that we're too bad to pray. Nevertheless, we must pray and keep on praying.

Famous 19th Century pastor and preacher, Charles Haddon Spurgeon, once said:

"...if you cannot pray, pray till you can." [4]

Are we struggling at this very moment? Then pray. Commit everything into God's hands, for He is more willing than we often think, to step into our world, into our corner, into our strife and to share our burdens. When God steps in, the result is Heaven touching earth; Heaven touching *your* earth and Heaven touching *my* earth. What better thing than *Heaven* touching us in a time of adversity!? That surely would be most precious. More precious in fact than anything this world has to offer. So tell God everything. Don't hold back. Be honest. Do you struggle to believe? Then tell Him. Are you falling apart? Then tell Him!

Jesus taught many things about prayer in his sermon on the mount:

"Ask, and it will be given to you; seek, and you will find; knock, and it will be opened to you. For everyone who asks receives, and he who seeks finds, and to him who knocks it will be opened. Or what man is there among you who, if his son asks for bread, will give him a stone? Or if he asks for a fish, will he give him a serpent? If you then, being evil, know how to give good gifts to your children, how much more will your Father who is in heaven give good things to those who ask him!" (Matthew 7:7-11)

Jesus placed a great deal of emphasis upon *asking*; He made the point five times in the above passage alone. He exhorted us to ask and keep on asking… and there is more than a measure of truth in the age-old saying, "If you don't ask – you don't get".

A story recorded in Luke's Gospel, commonly referred to as the Parable of the Unjust Judge, perfectly illustrates perseverance and persistence in prayer.

"Then He spoke a parable to them, that men always ought to pray and not lose heart, saying: 'There was in a certain city a judge who did not fear God nor regard man. Now there was a widow in that city; and she came to him, saying, 'Get justice for me from my adversary.' And he would not for a while; but afterward he said within himself, 'Though I do not fear God nor regard man, yet because this widow troubles me I will avenge her, lest by her continual coming

she weary me.' Then the Lord said, 'Hear what the unjust judge said, and shall God not avenge His own elect who cry out day and night to Him, though He bears long with them? I tell you that He will avenge them speedily. Nevertheless, when the Son of Man comes, will He really find faith on earth?'" (Luke18:1–8)

Matthew Henry's 'Commentary on the Whole Bible in One Volume', says of this parable:

"Christ shows, by a parable, the power of importunity among men. He gives you an instance of an honest cause that succeeded before an unjust judge, not by the equity or compassionableness of it, but purely by dint of importunity" [5]

Importunity is a word I used to dislike, probably because I didn't fully understand its meaning. Erroneously, I thought it meant requesting out of great want; I objected strongly to such a concept. I didn't want a God who merely answered prayer when people were in dire straits, impoverished or in great need; it seemed to be patronizing to me.

Its meaning, however, is something quite different. According to the Oxford Quick Reference Dictionary the definition is:

"Making persistent or pressing requests" [6]

Importunity is not about the woman's prevalent *need* as I had thought, but about the woman's *persistence* prevailing over the judge. In His parable, Jesus was focusing not so much on the pressing need of the woman, (for the judge in His story could not have cared less) but upon the woman's persistence.

Persistence in prayer is essential.

The story in the following chapter of this book is a perfect illustration of persistence and perseverance in prayer. The parents prayed, the family prayed and the local church prayed and God answered with a miracle.

Therefore, ask and keep on asking. Don't give up, be persistent, be constant and persevere. Ask and keep on asking, pray and keep on praying. *"For everyone who asks receives, and he who seeks finds, and to him who knocks it will be opened." (Matthew 7:8)*

Heavenly Father, now I begin to see the importance of prayer. Show me how I may draw near to You and turn my prayers into a lifeline for others. Amen. (Prayer written by Rob Giles 2014)

5

Esther's Story: God of Miracles!

"Trust in the Lord with all your heart, and lean not on your own understanding." (Proverbs 3:5) "For you formed my inward parts; you covered me in my mother's womb. I will praise You, for I am fearfully and wonderfully made; marvellous are your works, and that my soul knows very well." (Psalm 139:13&14).

Diagnosed with Severe Combined Immunodeficiency, baby Esther's life was in jeopardy. Most babies with this condition die within the first year, unless treated. The only successful treatment to date is a bone marrow transplant. Her parents, Sam and Indu, both being doctors, were under no illusions. There would be a hard road ahead.

This is Esther's amazing passage to recovery and Sam and Indu's personal journey of faith in discovering a God of miracles.

Esther's mother, Indu, grew up in a Hindu family and first learned about Christianity when she was eight years old and started attending Sunday school with a friend. She remained prayerful over the years but only came to know Jesus a few years ago. "I do not know specifically when I started to trust Jesus", said Indu scouring her memory, "but I do know that He was working in me even before I knew and trusted Him completely. I met Sam, who grew up in a Christian family and we got married a few years later. The bumpiest part of our journey of faith was when our second daughter Esther was diagnosed with a rare disease called Severe Combined Immunodeficiency."

Esther was but a few weeks old when she was diagnosed at a local paediatric hospital with this illness.

Severe Combined Immunodeficiency (SCID) is a rare genetic disorder in which both 'arms' of the adaptive immune system (B cells and T cells) are impaired. SCID is a severe form of immunodeficiency in which the immune system's ability to fight infectious diseases is seriously compromised to the point where it is considered almost nonexistent. SCID is also known as Bubble Boy Disease, coined from the story of David Philip Vetter who lived almost his entire life in a bubble-shaped sterile environment at the Texas Children's Hospital, Houston, Texas, USA. He died in 1984 aged 12 after an unsuccessful bone marrow transplant. His story became popular with the media and he became known as The Boy in the Plastic Bubble with a TV movie of the same name starring John Travolta and Glynnis O'Connor.

As physicians themselves, Sam and Indu started to research the illness. Very quickly they realised they were helpless without a bone-marrow transplant for Esther. Esther was released home from hospital after one week. Then, over the following weeks, Sam, Indu and baby Esther attended various clinics; it wasn't a straightforward illness. Esther was put on a variety of treatments. Her case was then referred to a SCID specialist and Esther was put on a bone-marrow transplant list. Esther's sister had blood tests to see if she was a match but unfortunately she wasn't and so the hospital had to search more extensively for donors. Esther didn't have any unusual genes, so the specialists were reasonably confident of finding a match. Indu said, "We felt slightly more relaxed after that."

Every few weeks Sam and Indu were being notified of potential donors, which lifted their spirits. However, when the donors were recalled for further testing, there was no match. This sequence of events went on for several months. "It was a very difficult thing to be at the end of the phone waiting for the call", said Indu. "I was praying about it the whole time, asking the Lord for provision that a bone-marrow donor might be found… that's what we desperately needed!"

When asked, "How did it transpire that the Church became involved in praying?" Indu replied, "The Church was involved in prayer right from the beginning. The evening that Esther fell ill and was admitted to hospital, I contacted the pastor's wife. I knew the mums and toddlers were meeting the following morning so I sent her a text saying, 'Can you pray with the mums; we're in hospital and we're not sure what's happening?' The following evening, the elders came to the hospital to pray with Esther and anointed her with oil. (*"Is any among you sick? Let him call for the elders of the Church, and let them pray over him, anointing him with oil in the name of the Lord. And the prayer of faith will save the sick, and the Lord will raise him up..." James 5:14&15).* They were absolute prayer 'warriors'. Later, when we informed James, our pastor, that Esther was to be put on a list for a bone-marrow transplant, he exclaimed, (probably in response to those verses from James 5) 'That's not right!' And after that he and the Church began praying for a miracle and complete healing."

While the Church continued to pray, there were still demanding practicalities in Esther's care. Whenever Indu carried out the infusion procedure for immunity cells, she had to keep Esther still - a difficult task as babies like to wriggle around. Esther had needles, one in each leg, and had to be kept still for an hour and a half while the infusion ran through. Indu found that putting Esther in the pushchair and taking her for a walk was the easiest way of keeping her still and quiet.

"Amy, one of the youth leaders from our Church", Indu recalled, "sent me a text message saying, 'I feel that the Lord is going to open up the skies and give you His light'. (To this day, she doesn't know why she sent me that message!) When the text came through, I was just going through the front door with the pushchair and it looked as though it was going to rain. I began to walk and the clouds opened up in front of me and the sunshine came right through into my garden. And as I walked, the sunshine seemed to follow me. I couldn't believe it! I thought to myself, 'This is amazing; this is NOT a coincidence!' It was January, and the snow was at its worst, and yet throughout I had dry weather and sunshine in which to walk Esther. I never had to use the rain cover on any occasion; not one drop of rain or flake of snow fell on her pushchair."

As a family unit, Sam, Indu, grandparents and

close relatives, all longed desperately for a transplant on behalf of Esther, or else they might lose her…that was the reality. There were still uncertainties though. Even if she were fortunate enough to have a transplant, she still might die. The mortality rate is so high with this particular illness.

Several months passed without any potential donors coming forward. However, the Church at Chawn Hill called for a day of prayer and fasting. The whole Church fasted and prayed. Sam and Indu's family, extended family and friends, likewise fasted and prayed for Esther on the same day.

"Everyone was praying for complete healing!" exclaimed Indu, "It sounded far-fetched to us because we're both physicians…"

"Throughout this period we had to keep Esther isolated. We weren't allowed to take her out for fear of her picking up an infection. But when she was about eight months old, we decided to have her dedicated [similar to christening but without the element of baptism]. We wanted to place her, by faith, into God's hands. We shouldn't really have taken her into a Church environment, because of her need for isolation, but we took her anyway… trusting the outcome to God. Everyone was praying for her and we felt so encouraged, encouraged too by the Scriptures and by the words that people were receiving for her."

During those long months when the prayer meetings were held at Chawn Hill Church, Indu being a young Christian, had been trying to understand the different names of Jehovah, such as: Jehovah rapha, *the Lord our healer* and Jehovah jireh, *the Lord our provider*, etc, etc. Indu sensed there was power in the names of 'Jehovah' and desired to learn more about them. "I thought," she said, "if only I could declare these names over Esther, it would be miraculous. So, with my 'i-Pad', I tried to download a table of all the different names and their meaning. There I was with my crying child, who wanted her next feed, and the download was going to take about twenty minutes. In frustration I thought to myself, 'I have no time for this!' So I proceeded to feed Esther and switched on the TV to watch one of the religious channels. Benny Hin was preaching and teaching; his talk was on *all the names of Jehovah*! I was flabbergasted! 'Lord!' I exclaimed, 'this is not just any old message - this is something I really need to take in!'"

"I recorded the programme, and was able to go through it again and check each and every Scripture for myself. Benny said, 'To have provision, you have to have vision – vision of Christ.'"

"At that time I'd been thinking about Anna, a prophetess of the New Testament. She had been waiting for the coming of the Messiah throughout her long, long life. She just waited on God – and turned out to be one of the first, and one of only a handful, to recognise that this baby, Jesus, was indeed the saviour of the world. For some reason I kept thinking to myself: 'This is it, this is it; we just have to wait on the Lord and He will deliver us!'"

Indu decided that even as a doctor, she was first and foremost a child of God and a mother... and so together, she and Sam turned to Jesus for divine healing.

Sam and Indu had an appointment to see the main consultant at a tertiary paediatric hospital in

London. On the way there, Indu spoke to Sam about the different names of Jehovah and what Benny Hin had said on the TV; 'To have provision we need to have vision'. "Sam" she said, "I believe the Lord wants us to pray for complete healing. There is just something about it at this point in time; I think she is healed." Sam replied, "Even as Christians we're not exempt from these things. We just have to deal with it. We can trust the Lord to be near us through it all, but we're not exempt from these things in life."

When they arrived at the hospital and sat in the consulting room they were informed that the medical team were unable to find a suitable donor. They'd searched extensively internationally, and had found no one having the same genetic make up. As one might expect, Sam and Indu were quite shocked to hear this report. Then the consultant said, "but there is an interesting thing taking place and I want to go over Esther's results with you'. Sam and Indu immediately sat up in their chairs. "Look at the trend of things!" the consultant explained, "this is how it was at the very bad, the very low levels - where she stopped making immunity cells etc; but there is this one little marker that comes up positive. We don't quite know what it is yet, but I think we need to monitor it because it might be something of significance."

"Both Sam and I looked at each other in almost disbelief! 'I'm sorry', said the consultant, 'I can't give you any more information, but let's just watch this and see what happens. You carry on doing what you are doing and we will see you again in a month.' We rose from the consultation, greatly encouraged. Sam was pushing the pushchair as we stepped outside; he looked at me and said, 'She's been healed!' There were tears in our eyes. After that we began giving thanks to the Lord, even before the doctors knew Esther was healed.

Two days later through the post, Indu received a cardboard tube with no return address, nor any indication of who had sent it. Unbelievably, it was a prayer mat and on it were all the names of Jehovah! Indu said, "It's now in Esther's room, because it's our testimony to the healing power and provision of God. It was just incredible, it really was, and I must say from that time on I had hope for every little thing. I could say with conviction, 'I trust You Lord and I know You are near us always.'"

"Months later," Indu continued, "the Hospital team were still unsure what the anomaly was they had found, but we just knew that Esther had started getting better. Our other daughter is a toddler and goes to nursery. She comes home with all manner of ailments and yet she hasn't managed to transfer anything to Esther! They play in the same room, they give cuddles and kisses, they share the same toys, they use the same cups to drink from and it's almost as though Esther has her own little 'bubble' around her! It's been quite bizarre. I've been poorly, Sam's been poorly and the child minder has been poorly, but Esther's been completely fine; somehow she's been protected through it all!"

The Hospital began cutting down on her treatment with each visit after she was a year old. Their purpose was to ascertain how her body was performing in connection with her own immunity. When Sam and Indu took her for one of her monthly appointments, the medical staff took an extensive series of blood tests. These showed there were still low levels of immunity but things appeared promising. The specialist arranged for more in-depth tests. He felt confident that she would show some sort of low levels of immunity.

"It was January," Indu enthused, "Friday the 13th to be precise, when we received a call in the evening from the Hospital. 'Esther has normal levels of immunity - the same levels as a normal child.'" Indu was flabbergasted, "Not even *low* levels; it was completely normal! It was just phenomenal!"

"Sam and I have seen miracles of medicine but we know this was no coincidence. This was *our Maker* at work. Esther didn't possess the normal mechanism within her body to produce these types of cells. Miraculously her body was able to mount a response despite not having the appropriate mechanism. I still recall one of the consultants saying, 'Yes! It's miraculous! Isn't it?' Sam and I sometimes sit together and muse about what has happened. We go 'Wow! What an awesome God!' When we see her running around being mischievous, we go, 'Wow! Look at all of this: such mercy, such grace, it's wonderful; it's completely supernatural.'"

> *Father God I thank You for the gift of this child. I thank You that she is 'fearfully and wonderfully made' as David said in the Psalms. I thank You for performing your amazing miracle of healing. As she grows I pray that she will grow into a fine young woman, ready to help those in need. I pray that every year that has been extended to her life will be made to count for your kingdom. I ask this in the name of Jesus Christ our Lord. Amen. (Prayer written by Rob Giles 2014)*

6

A Question of Suffering

"The steps of a good man are ordered by the Lord, and He delights in his way. Though he fall, he shall not be utterly cast down; for the Lord upholds him with His hand." (Psalm 37:23&24)

God is a God of the supernatural - a God of miracles. He often performs miracles in our lives and answers our prayers on a daily basis but on occasion we fail to recognise them. Sometimes we receive answers to our prayers and at other times we do not. Sometimes God answers with an amazing miracle as with baby Esther and at other times there are no answers. Things may even appear to go from bad to worse. So I ask: "What does happen when we do not receive the answer we desire?" At such times we may feel like asking several deep, searching questions, "Has something gone wrong?" "Is there something wrong with me?" "Has God let me down?" or "Has my faith failed?" I think not.

Life dishes out rubbish. It doesn't matter who we are, whether we are Christian or not. Nor does it matter if we are a Jew, Muslim, Hindu, Buddhist, Sikh or atheist; no one is exempt from suffering. I am of course stating the obvious.

We live in a fallen world in which trouble, strife, heartache, illness and pain are no respecters of persons. Affliction crosses all barriers and breaks all defences. Wealth, rank or position cannot grant immunity. Doctors, pharmacists and scientists cannot stave it off. Politicians cannot legislate against it. Barristers and lawyers cannot litigate against it. Hardship strikes the rich, the poor and the famous. It buffets the good and the bad and is not confined solely to the elderly. Neither are unborn babes guaranteed a safe passage from the womb to their mothers' arms. Nor are they guaranteed immunity from deformity or disability. Infants and young children may also develop life-threatening illnesses, for there is no indemnity. It is a sad, sad fact of life; as the Bible puts it, *"... man is born to trouble, as the sparks fly upward" (Job 5:7).*

When suffering comes our way we often say things such as: "Why? Why me!? I don't 'deserve' this!" "This thing has wrecked my plans and ruined my life!" Let's be honest, there are times when we all think we deserve better. Furthermore, when we see kind, helpful and generous souls suffering in great affliction, we are readily enraged. We may be even more disturbed when we discover someone who is nothing but a wastrel or a bone-idle scrounger, enjoying good health and seemingly living life to the full!

Life often appears to be unfair. In the Psalms,

David, too, struggled to come to terms with the same apparent injustices of life:

"For I was envious of the boastful, when I saw the prosperity of the wicked. For there are no pangs in their death, but their strength is firm. They are not in trouble as other men, nor are they plagued like other men..." (Psalm 73:3-5)

At times, this apparent inequity really does 'hack us off'. I've heard people say when they see a bad person in health, 'riding high' and 'living it up': 'I've lived my life for nothing; I might just as well have been rotten to the core for all the good it's done me!' or, 'If I were God, I'd want to share things out more fairly than this!' Or they might go even further and retort: 'I say *blow* the wicked! Let the *contemptible* suffer and let the *good* walk free!' No doubt we've all heard people express similar sentiments; possibly we've even thought as much ourselves. Of course, such comments seem quite reasonable and do have a certain 'equitable' or even 'justifiable' ring to them. In an ideal world it would be rather satisfying to most of us if the wicked were the ones who suffered rather than the good. Unfortunately we do not live in an ideal world.

We've all heard the saying, "The sun always shines on the righteous". Well, you don't have to work for the Meteorological Office to realise that it doesn't! Jesus said: *"...for He makes His sun rise on the evil and on the good, and sends rain on the just and on the unjust."* (Matthew 5:45).

This existence of ours is far from ideal, far from fair and far from perfect. Life dishes out garbage but it's not the type of garbage we can gather up and deposit in a refuse sack. Although we'd dearly love to at times, more

Where Heaven Touches Earth

often than not we have to live with, and work through, whatever comes our way. As Sam said to Indu, 'Even as Christians, we're not exempt from these things. We just have to deal with them. We can trust the Lord to be near us through it all.' There is more than just a grain of truth in that statement.

Suffering, however, does play a major role in life. We may not want to hear that sort of message – nevertheless it is true.

There is a verse of Scripture that some Christians tend to quote rather glibly. Often it is quoted in a very patronising way and comes over like a slap in the face to those who are suffering. The 'controversial' verse in question is this:

"And we know that all things work together for good to those who love God, to those who are the called according to His purpose."(Romans 8:28)

It's not nice when insensitive folk quote that verse. Nonetheless, the truth of those words can give assurance and bring a great deal of comfort to those who are struggling. Personally speaking, I have received comfort, support and a great deal of assurance from that verse. The assurance is in knowing that God cares, that He hasn't been caught off guard; the comfort is in knowing that He is with me; the support is in knowing nothing escapes His notice and nothing is worthless in His economy. For *"...all things work together for good." (Romans 8:28)*

Use of the word *purpose* in the Bible is fascinating. The Greek New Testament word for purpose is *prosthesis* [7] and is used only twelve times in the NT, one of which is in Romans 8:28. Literally it means 'setting before' or 'setting forth'. Of the twelve, eight generally refer to God's eternal purpose in salvation, i.e. a well laid out master plan. Of the remaining four, *prosthesis* is used in relation to the Levitical showbread, literally translated the bread of 'setting before', the bread of 'His presence' or the bread of 'His purpose'. You could call it the 'purpose bread'.

Jesus, of course, is the living embodiment of that bread. He is the bread of life, the bread of heaven: *"I am the living bread which came down from heaven. If anyone eats of this bread, he will live forever..." (John 6:51)* The bread that we break and partake of at communion represents His body broken for us, i.e. the bread of 'setting before', the bread of 'His purpose'. There is an element of *suffering* attached to the word *prosthesis*.

I believe God has a purpose in everything that takes place in our lives. From our point of view His purposes are an 'offering' which we offer to God, which we partake of and identify with as being our… oneness with the bread of heaven. There will be times, however, when we may have great difficulty in spotting *that* purpose for ourselves. At such times we must simply entrust our lives and our situation to God. Other times we may find that God is able to turn the mess we're in into something beautiful, something that will transform our lives and deepen our relationship with Him *"...to give them beauty for ashes, the oil of joy for mourning, the garment of praise for the spirit of heaviness..." (Isaiah 61:3).* God has a purpose in everything - nothing is wasted. For we learn far more in the adversities of life than in any mountain-top experience.

There are many Christians who have found God to be with them in the most difficult and trying of circumstances. Some have gone through all manner of tragedies and yet remain radiant. It's my guess we've all met one or two of these beautiful people and wondered, "What is their secret?" That secret, I believe, is in discovering that 'God is with us' as demonstrated so dramatically in their stories.

God is with us – is a phenomenon we will learn firsthand through the difficult experiences of life. As the psalmist said (in reflection), *"Before I was afflicted I went astray, but now I keep Your word. (Psalm 119:67)* In testing times, few people would claim to feel the presence of God from the outset. It's often later upon looking back we discover that God had been with us all the time. It's then we recognise that the unseen hand of God had supported us throughout.

Although we may *fall* into despair, depression, sorrow and grief, and experience tribulation, suffering and pain, the following Scripture text gives us an amazing promise; *"Though he fall, he shall not be utterly cast down; for the Lord upholds him with His hand." (Psalm 37:24)* There is a way through our sufferings, difficulties and hardships with God at our side. That is the reality.

Tim Hughes, in his worship song *'Be my everything'* [8], brings home the point that *God is with us* in everything. Tim points out that God is with us in every aspect of our lives, including our low points, when we weep and when we hurt.

Are we able to believe the promises of God? Are we able to trust Him to uphold us with His hand? If we are, then we are truly in a place where heaven touches earth. Can we, indeed, place our hand in the hand of our Saviour, the Lord Jesus Christ, and discern that He is there at our side? I sincerely hope so.

Rob Giles

O Lord, as I quiet myself to contemplate the universal reality of adversity and suffering, open the eyes of my heart to the authenticity of Your nearness and support. Help me to discover through experience that You are at my side, never to leave me, never to forsake me. Assist me in making this vital connection with You that will lead me to intimacy. I ask this, in and through the name of Jesus, Amen. (Prayer written by Rob Giles 2014)

7

Pray: Praying For Others

"...pray for one another, that you may be healed. The effective, fervent prayer of a righteous man avails much." (James 5:16) "But when He saw the multitudes, He was moved with compassion for them...Then He said to His disciples, 'The harvest truly is plentiful, but the labourers are few. Therefore pray the Lord of the harvest to send out labourers into His harvest.'" (Matthew 9:36-38)

Praying for others is right at the heart of the Christian faith. The Scriptures encourage us to pray for each other, *"...pray for one another, that you may be healed. The effective, fervent prayer of a righteous man avails much."* (James 5:16) Praying for others is something that all of us can do, if we so choose.

Praying for someone other than ourselves can be difficult at times, as we have already seen. For instance, if you have lost a loved one, the last thing on your mind will be to think of someone else. And again if you lose your job, pass through a period of depression or meet with financial difficulty, these things can make us feel lonely, anxious and isolated. To some extent we become self-absorbed and wrapped in our own world of woe. In these circumstances it may be very difficult to think of others, let alone pray for them.

Christianity is not easy...for Christianity demands an element of self-denial. *Self-denial in action* will, however, help lift us out of our world of woe by meeting our troubles head on - if we have the courage to allow *self-denial* to do so.

To illustrate, allow me to share from my own experience.

When I broke down, I broke down in the main due to stress and eventually I lost my secular job. I was deemed to have left my place of employment of my own volition, so I was unable to receive benefit (specifically Job Seekers Allowance). This was the point at which I was personally challenged by those two little words - *self-denial*. I felt that I needed to step out in faith in an attempt to meet my difficulties head on.

I began by using my own trouble to pray for others. For instance, a gentleman at our Church had lost his job... now this I could relate to. I thought of the similar situation I was in - I thought of the stress losing my job had caused me. I thought of the fear that had come over me; "How will we get by?" "Where will the money come from?" "What about this...?" and "What about that...?" When I prayed about those things I chose not to pray for my *own* need, but rather I prayed for *his* need instead... this was the self-denial step I felt God wanted me to take. It seemed radical, but I simply added a postscript to my prayer, *"Lord, don't forget me in this, Amen"*.

I have to confess, it wasn't at all easy to pray for someone other than me, particularly when I was overcome with my own hurt. I really had a tussle to deny myself the luxury of praying for myself. But I made it my aim that every time I was conscious of my own pressing need and subsequent fears, I would pray for him instead.

Over a period of time, I was amazed to find that God brought me and my wife through that dark time. By the same token, those whom I had prayed had also been blessed. I discovered too, that God had quite naturally led me into an aspect of *watching*. Prior to this experience, I had no idea what watching was all about. Through the way of praying I've outlined to you, I became aware that I was actively *watching* out for people who were in a similar predicament to me. This was an amazing concept. Some time later, however, God showed me another aspect of watching.

One night I awoke in the small hours of the morning, shivering - the first signs of a chill. I could not get warm. I went downstairs and put the fire on. I put on a fleece jacket (on top of my dressing gown) and wrapped myself in a blanket. As I sat in silence with the lights off I began to pray. I allowed my mind to wander to the homeless... firstly I began praying for them.

Then my mind latched onto yesterday's international news... the massive earthquake in Pakistan! I thought of the thousands of homeless, living in mere tents in the mountains, facing the prospect of an atrocious winter. My own discomfort had become the key to leading me into a period of intercession. This episode took place *during the night* - it was a revelation to me. It was praying during the *night-watches* just as the Bible had instructed.

It is my experience that if we will put ourselves out just a little and pray for people other than ourselves, in the way I have suggested, we will become more thoughtful and less self-absorbed. God will also be at liberty to develop compassion in our hearts. I don't know if you are anything like me, but I do not find it easy to love people - I mean love people with true Christian love. My wife, on the other hand, is a great lover of people, very thoughtful and very caring.

We read much in the New Testament about Christian love; sadly very few of us appear to possess this great quality. Jesus said, *"A new commandment I give to you, that you love one another; as I have loved you, that you also love one another. By this all will know that you are my disciples, if you have love for one another."* *(John13:34&35)*

I have to confess, Christian love does not come at all easy to me. Over the forty plus years I have been a Christian I've heard many sermons on Christian love, and I guess we've all heard many speakers give talks on the topic. But as far as I am aware, I have never heard one message on how we might develop Christian love when we do not possess it. For me, the answer came through this way of praying.

I found it quite astonishing that compassion was developing in my heart through simply praying in the way I have described. The more I *watched* – my family, friends, neighbours, the Church, the news etc and prayed - the more I was moved with compassion. The more I was moved with compassion - the more I prayed and the more I watched.

Intercession is something that none of us needs to be afraid off. I have found that the best way to approach intercessory prayer is just to come before God without an agenda. Simply turn up and worship Him. Take the simple steps of *self-denial* in prayer as I have suggested and ask God to take you deeper. If God desires us to intercede, then He will open the way; if all that's needed is simply to spend five minutes praying for someone, then nothing is lost. At least this way we're not trying to force or contrive anything. All that God requires of us is that we turn up and 'go with the flow' of the Holy Spirit.

A further aspect of intercession is what I call *carrying a burden*. This is where God lays a burden upon the heart and we carry that burden in prayer until the Lord answers one way or the other and the burden lifts. This may sound a little highfaluting - but it's not. It is simpler than we might think. Again, allow me to share a little more from my own experience. It is a rather disgusting example - for which I apologise - but this is what actually took place.

I had a bad case of diarrhoea, an excessive loss in energy and felt desperately ill. Following the pattern of prayer that I've described, I began praying seriously for places such as Africa, where there are many cases of diarrhoea, dysentery and water-borne diseases, due to contaminated water and poor sanitation. I prayed for anything associated with diarrhoea (pardon the thought!) I could think of. I did this as a matter of course (my prayer strategy) even though I didn't think for one moment that I was suffering from an actual water-borne disease myself!

I have a chronic illness called fibromyalgia which causes me to experience similar symptoms to the ones described, so it took me several days before I was convinced that I needed to consult my doctor. Samples, of course, were sent away for analysis as usual.

During the time I was ill, a major disaster (a tsunami) occurred. So, I began praying into that situation also, praying particularly against an outbreak of cholera. Whenever I felt ill during the day, I prayed. A substantial amount of my praying took place during the night, particularly in the small hours of the morning (because I couldn't sleep). Many of my prayers were *groans that cannot be uttered* with *tears* as I cried out to God. It was a period when a burden came upon me from God (although I was unaware of it initially). I decided that I would carry this burden upon my heart for the duration of my illness. I had never before experienced a period of prayer of this magnitude, and one which lasted in total around three weeks. When I was with people, the burden lifted but as soon as I was alone, the burden returned and I was praying in tears in a matter of moments.

It turned out that I was praying against cholera long before it became a genuine concern... and long before the first cases became international news. There was an outbreak of cholera but it was contained, and never reached the epidemic proportions expected. I cannot claim that my prayers averted an epidemic... but it was good to see the hand of God so clearly at work, and it was good to feel that I had played a small role in God's plan.

After recovery, I was surprised when I received a 'phone call from Environmental Health (EH) saying that I had contracted *cryptosporidium*, a highly contagious water-borne parasite, but I was an isolated case. (I had been working on a barge and dropped a tool into the canal. I put my hand into the murky water and retrieved the tool. With no satisfactory means of washing my hands I later ate my lunch.) I was amazed; God had kept me safe through the illness... and God had protected everyone around me! Praise God!

I want to make it absolutely clear – I am no great praying man; I'm just an ordinary kind of guy. But God can use anyone. All we have to do is make ourselves available. At that time I was a broken soul battling against depression and alcoholism. And some of what I have shared took place before God broke the power of alcoholism in my life. Yes, I can't work that one out either!

When I look back, I now recognise that the aspects of prayer I have shared with you were all part and parcel of God's recovery plan for my life. The prayer strategy that God had shown me played a remarkable role in my recovery from the breakdown, from my depression and from the power of alcoholism. This was God's way of not allowing me to be overcome by my circumstances, but of overcoming my circumstances by meeting them head-on in prayer.

Out of this *simple* prayer strategy, I discovered that compassion for people was beginning to develop in my heart. This phenomenon at first surprised me, for I had not set out with that objective in mind. I quickly realised, however, that prayer changes things even though God may not directly answer the prayers we pray.

Once you catch a glimpse of compassion developing, don't let it go; build on it. The Apostle Paul said: *"But above all these things put on love, which is the bond of perfection." (Colossians 3:14)* Do as Paul said;

put on love, don't wait around for it to come to you. Put it on and do the loving thing.

> *Lord Jesus, teach me to pray. Teach me to view people as You see them, that is, with the eyes of love and compassion. Grant me the grace to think of others even when my own back is to the wall. This was Your way; make it my way, through Jesus Christ our Lord Amen. (Prayer written by Rob Giles 2014)*

8

Pray: Without Words

"And you will seek Me and find Me, when you search for Me with all your heart." (Jeremiah 29:13) When You said, 'Seek my face,' my heart said to You, 'Your face, Lord, I will seek.'" (Psalm 27:8) "...but the Spirit Himself makes intercession for us with groanings which cannot be uttered." (Romans 8:26)

Without words, "What is meant by such a title?"

Without words is simply taking a closer look at silent forms of prayer.

Prayer is one of the noblest activities a Christian may perform, but for many of us, prayer does not come at all easily.

We may ask, "Why should that be?" "What are the reasons?"

The speed of life, for one, will contribute greatly to a breakdown in private prayer and devotion. Most of us have busy schedules and we race from one thing to another in an attempt to cram as much into the evaporating hours as we possibly can. The pace of life is such that we must prioritise, thus leaving some things undone. 'tough luck', we say, 'I can't be in two places at once!' Prayer will often suffer as a consequence.

Preachers exhort us to make time. We're left thinking, "How?" If you are a busy working mum, for example, you might just as well be a juggler with all the balls you have to keep in the air. Finding time to fit something in is not at all easy but if that *something* is important, worthwhile or enjoyable enough, we will make time for it. However, prayer is not often high on our list of important, worthwhile and enjoyable activities. You may be wondering, "What then can be done?"

Bizarrely, this is where our trials and the difficulties of life may come to our rescue. The difficulties we face will either drive us away from God or they will drive us closer to Him. If we are troubled by the trials we endure and seek God in prayer, then those trials will have served a greater purpose. Not a pleasant purpose I know, but a very significant one indeed.

We can become enslaved within a trial, both by resisting and by attempting to wriggle out of it. There are times, however, when we must go through a trial for our own good. Peter tells us in his first letter, that God has *begotten* us to a living hope through the resurrection of Jesus Christ, to an incorruptible inheritance that is reserved for us in heaven and that we are kept by the power of God through faith. Then he utters these remarkable words.

"In this you greatly rejoice, though now for a little while, if need be, you have been grieved by various trials, that the genuineness of your faith, being much more precious than gold that perishes, though it be tested with fire, may be found

to praise, honour, and glory at the revelation of Jesus Christ."
(1 Peter 1:6&7)

Around the turn of the millennium, I suffered a mental and emotional breakdown. Sadly, I turned to alcohol in order to cope, which actually created more problems for me than the breakdown itself. That period of my life was very dark but it did drive me to God in prayer. Because I felt 'lost' and 'undone', and did not seem to possess the mental prowess to perform certain tasks, I began to converse with God in a way I had never done before.

With God, I rehearsed almost every activity that I needed to do, talking each one through with Him in prayer and then prayerfully performing what needed to be done. This was a great lesson for me to learn. And yet, it was only part of the story.

When you are in a broken state, it can be very difficult to pray for other people. My prayer-life seemed to be very inadequate. My prayers felt useless even though I was praying more than I had ever done. The feelings of 'falling short' and of 'missing the mark' were quite overwhelming and those feelings only added to my depression. My response, however, was not to allow myself to sink deeper and deeper but to *seek* God, in order to overcome my depression. In answer, God showed me that there was far more to prayer than mere words.

Discovering there is more to prayer than words has been one of the greatest revelations I have received about prayer. There is a strong case for words not always being necessary. Prayers which may or may not be constructed with words include: intercessions made with groanings that cannot be uttered, tears, waiting, beholding, meditating, watching and contemplating. By way of introduction, let us look at these seven a little closer.

What of intercessions made with groanings which cannot be uttered?

These are intercessions where we are burdened but cannot find the words to express what we want to say. So we groan... With the aid of the Holy Spirit our groans can be turned into prayers. Paul said, *"Likewise the Spirit also helps in our weaknesses. For we do not know what we should pray for as we ought, but the Spirit Himself makes intercession for us with groanings which cannot be uttered. Now He who searches the hearts knows what the mind of the Spirit is, because He makes intercession for the saints according to the will of God." (Romans 8:26&27)*

The phrase, *'which cannot be uttered'*, can be good news for those whose lives are broken. Knowing that the Holy Spirit is alongside, praying with you, praying through you (even though you can't find the words) will be like medicine to the soul.

What then of tears?

Tears, particularly for men, are often perceived as a sign of weakness. They need not be - for tears themselves can be prayers in their own right. God said through Isaiah, *"...I have heard your prayer, I have seen your tears; surely I will heal you..." (2 Kings 20:5)* The Psalmist said, *"Hear my prayer, O Lord, and give ear to my cry; do not be silent at my tears..." (Psalm 39:12)* and, *"You number my wanderings; put my tears into Your bottle; are they not in Your book? When I cry out to You, then my enemies will turn back; this I know, because God is for me." (Psalm 56:8&9)*

These verses suggest that tears may be prayers in

their own right. God keeps our tears as a memorial, *in a bottle*, and writes them *in His book*. You might ask, "How can tears be written - other than to record that so-and-so cried on such a day?" No, God interprets them! Therefore our tears speak to Him. For the Christian, tears are not cried in vain. God will not forget our tears... not until that great day when He will wipe away all tears from our eyes. *(see Isaiah 25:8, Revelation 7:17 & Revelation 21:4)*

That tears may be prayers is more good news for those who are broken and for those who cannot put their grief into words. Tears often flow from the heart, and God reads the heart; nothing escapes Him. Therefore, tears can be prayers.

What about waiting?

The most famous verses on *waiting* are found in Isaiah 40 and are cited often by Christians, *"But those who wait on the Lord shall renew their strength; they shall mount up with wings like eagles, they shall run and not be weary, they shall walk and not faint." (Isaiah 40:31)*

Waiting on God is a type of prayer which, to a large extent, has been lost from our storehouse of prayer. Waiting is largely silent, seeking, reflective, and can also be an expression of contemplative prayer.

Another expression of *waiting* prayer was revived by the Moravians and Puritans; later, it became the main form of worship for John Fox and the Quakers. Waiting on God featured heavily in the Welsh revival and in the Azusa Street revival of California, where Christians waited on God by seeking Him in silent prayer for the outpouring of the Holy Spirit. This played a vibrant part in early Pentecostalism with 'waiting meetings', sometimes called 'tarrying meetings', where groups of believers waited for the Holy Spirit to come in power.

Many great leaders such as George Whitfield, John Wesley, Charles Finney, George and Stephen Jeffries and Smith Wigglesworth *waited* on God; it was the means by which these men of God received their power in ministry, prophecy, words of knowledge, healings and miracles.

Periods of silent waiting can also be incorporated into intercessory prayer, where participants *wait* for an answer from God.

We would do well to seize every opportunity to delve deeper into this powerful phenomenon by restoring waiting to our repertoire of prayer. *"Wait on the Lord; be of good courage, And He shall strengthen your heart; Wait, I say, on the Lord!" (Psalm 27:14)*

What then of beholding?

You might ask, "What part does beholding play in prayer?" The Psalmist said; *"One thing I have desired of the Lord, that will I seek: That I may dwell in the house of the Lord all the days of my life, to behold the beauty of the Lord, and to inquire in His temple." (Psalm 27:4)*

In the above verse the psalmist seeks the presence of God and desires to dwell in God's house all the days of his life. Now the psalmist is not speaking literally of being in Church every day, but of practising the presence of God and of living in constant communion with Him. This is a high goal indeed, but one that I believe to be very much attainable by those who seek.

Beholding is a silent, worshipful means of prayer. The person praying this way rests in the presence of God, reverently and worshipfully giving their love to Him. They gaze in faith with the eyes of the spirit upon the beauty of Jesus Christ. This way of praying may also be an aspect of contemplative prayer as we shall see in a later study.

What about meditation?

Some Christians confuse Christian meditation with transcendental meditation and Far Eastern religions. However, Christian meditation has nothing remotely to do with those practices. Trevor Dearing, charismatic Anglican minister and author of *Meditate And Be Made Whole Through Jesus Christ* asserts:

"It is to whom one prays that is of fundamental importance...it is upon what one meditates that is of vital importance for specifically Christian meditation." (9)

Meditation is found extensively throughout the Bible. It refers in the main to meditating on the Scriptures. God encouraged Joshua to practise it. *(see Joshua 1:8)*

Reference to meditation appears fifteen times in the Psalms and seven times in Psalm 119 alone. The first Psalm says, *"...his delight is in the law of the Lord, and in His law he meditates day and night." (Psalm 1:2)*

Paul instructed Timothy to meditate, *"...give attention to reading, to exhortation, to doctrine. Do not neglect the gift that is in you, which was given to you by prophecy with the laying on of the hands of the eldership. Meditate on these things... (1Timothy 4:13-15)* Paul was doubtless speaking of the Scriptures when he referred to reading, exhortation and doctrine.

Christian meditation therefore, is meditating upon the Scriptures, the Bible. The Psalmist said, *"I will meditate on Your precepts, and contemplate Your ways. I will delight myself in Your statutes; I will not forget Your word." (Psalm 119:15&16)* Meditation is prayerful, reflective and objective thought upon the Scriptures and is a powerful means of renewing the mind. My view is this: take the Scriptures into your heart, meditate upon the Living Word and allow the Word to challenge, guide and transform your life.

What then of watching?

"Then He (Jesus) came to the disciples and found them sleeping, and said to Peter, 'What? Could you not watch with Me one hour? Watch and pray, lest you enter into temptation. The spirit indeed is willing, but the flesh is weak." (Matthew 26:40&41)

Watching is an aspect of prayer that many of us today have lost touch with. It is prayerfully keeping our eyes open. Another aspect of watching is staying awake or waking at some point during the night for prayer, meditation, contemplation or waiting on God.

The Psalmist said, *"When I remember You on my bed, I meditate on You in the night watches. Because You have been my help, therefore in the shadow of Your wings I will rejoice." (Psalm 63:6&7)* and *"My eyes are awake through the night watches, that I may meditate on Your word." (Psalm 119: 148)*

In his second letter to the Corinthians, Paul listed the hardships he had endured in serving Christ. On his list is this extraordinary verse, *"In toil and hardship, watching often [through sleepless nights], in hunger and thirst, frequently driven to fasting by want, in cold and exposure and lack of clothing. And besides those things that are without, there is the daily [inescapable pressure] of my care and anxiety for all the Churches!" (2 Corinthians 11:27&28. The Amplified Bible).*

Paul turned his sleepless nights into prayer; he turned his hunger and thirst into fasting and he turned his burden for the Churches into *watch-night* prayer. This was Paul's way of not being overcome by his circumstances, but rather of overcoming his circumstances by meeting them head-on in prayer. His example shows that it matters little whether we *deliberately choose* to watch, by setting aside a specific time for that purpose, or whether we are *pressed into it* by turning our sleepless nights into periods of watching. The important thing is that we welcome *watching* into our prayer routines.

A further aspect of *watching* that will help us view family, friends, the Church, the wider community and even the world in a different light is *watching* prayerfully for people's needs. This means keeping our eyes and ears prayerfully open, so that when we spot a need we are instantly praying. It's more than likely we will be among the first to be praying for that particular need. With a *watchful*, prayerful heart we may, by the Holy Spirit, anticipate things taking place long before they actually do. God may use our prayers to ward off dangers and even change a course of events through *watching*.

What then of contemplation?

This is but a brief introduction to contemplation as there are four chapters on the subject to follow. The act of contemplation, though simple, is vast, challenging and life-changing and cannot be dealt with in a few sentences. But what we will discover in the course of these studies is that contemplation will be a great tool in facing life's most difficult challenges.

Christian contemplation incorporates all the silent forms of prayer - and all the silent forms of prayer may be derived from contemplation. Like meditation, contemplation has received undue criticism, with some sections of the Church suggesting links to transcendental meditation and Far Eastern religions. It is thought that participants empty their minds, thus opening themselves up to demonic activity. However, this is far from the truth. In my experience participants *do not* empty their minds; rather they set their minds upon Jesus Christ. Isaiah said, *"You will keep him in perfect peace, whose mind is stayed on You, because he trusts in You." (Isaiah 26:3)* A mind stayed upon God should be one of the main objectives of those who practise contemplative prayer.

These seven, silent forms of prayer are all ways of seeking God on a personal and intimate level. It doesn't matter whether we can find the words to pray or not; simply come before God reverently, just as you are, for He reads our hearts. If you are finding it difficult to pray, it need not get you down - for God is closer than you think. Jesus understands the human heart because He Himself became human. He reads the meaning of your tears and your groanings. He longs to step into your sorrow, grief and pain, if you will only allow Him. Will you allow Him into your disconsolate heart?

Heavenly Father, thank You that I should no longer feel upset when I cannot find the words to pray; help me to recognise that You are closer than I often think. Enlighten me, equip me and teach me, using these simple prayerful techniques. Through Jesus Christ our Lord, I ask. Amen. (Prayer written by Rob Giles 2014)

9

Contemplative Prayer: The Principles

"I beseech you therefore, brethren, by the mercies of God, that you present your bodies a living sacrifice, holy, acceptable to God, which is your reasonable service. And do not be conformed to this world, but be transformed by the renewing of your mind, that you may prove what is that good and acceptable and perfect will of God."
(Romans 12:1&2)

"What is contemplative prayer or Christian contemplation?" For clarity, we must first turn to the dictionary. I have used several dictionaries in order to arrive at a more comprehensive definition. The Kindle dictionary defines contemplation as being: *"(a) the action of looking thoughtfully at something for a long time. (b) deep reflective thought."* The Collins Dictionary and Thesaurus says: *"1. to think about intently and at length. 2. to think intently and at length, esp. for spiritual reasons; meditate. 3. to look at thoughtfully."* The Oxford Quick Reference Dictionary's simple definition is: *"to survey intently, visually or mentally."* And Webster's Concise

English Dictionary defines it as: *"to look at steadily; to reflect upon, to meditate; to have in view."*

Bearing these quotes in mind, Christian contemplation then is *the action of looking thoughtfully* at Jesus Christ *for a long period of time.* It is *deep reflective thought* on Christ. It is *thinking about* the person of Jesus Christ *intently and at length, esp. for spiritual reasons;* to *meditate.* It is *to survey* Christ, His Father, His kingdom and His cross *intently* both *visually* (with the eyes of faith) *and mentally* (with the mind). It is *to look at* Jesus Christ *steadily; to reflect upon, to meditate; to have in view* His Person and Godhead. These, I believe, are the characteristics which truly define Christian contemplation.

The Apostle Paul wrote these words in his letter to the Colossians, revealing the supremacy of Christ:

"He (Jesus) is the image of the invisible God, the firstborn over all creation, for by Him all things were created that are in heaven and that are on earth, visible or invisible, whether thrones or dominions or principalities or powers. All things were created through Him and for Him. And He is before all things, and in Him all things consist. And He is the head of the body, the church, who is the beginning, the firstborn from the dead, that in all things He may have the pre-eminence. For it pleased the Father that in Him all the fullness should dwell, and by Him to reconcile all things to Himself, by Him whether things on earth or in heaven, having made peace through the blood of His cross." (Colossians 1:13-20)

If we would catch a glimpse of *the invisible God*, then we must gaze upon Jesus Christ through the eyes of faith, for *'He is the image of the invisible God'*. Jesus Himself said, *"No one comes to the Father except through Me." (John 14:6)*

When Philip said to Jesus, 'Lord, show us the Father'; Jesus replied by saying, *"Have I been with you so long, and yet you have not known Me, Philip? He who has seen Me has seen the Father; so how can you say, 'Show us the Father'?" (John 14:9)*

The Apostle Paul also wrote, *"For there is one God and one mediator between God and men, the man Christ Jesus, who gave Himself a ransom for all" (1Timothy 2:5).*

Early exponents of Christian contemplation all agree that Jesus Christ Himself is the object of contemplative prayer and that our focus should be upon Him.

Contemplative prayer depends then upon our focus. If we are to practise it as prescribed by the early Christian contemplatives, Jesus Christ *Himself* will be the object and focus of our prayer. In this respect, there is no difference between contemplative prayer and any other Christian prayer, for every true Christian prayer is presented to God the Father, *in* and *through* the name of Jesus Christ.

Whenever we pray in contemplation, it should always be to worship the Lord Jesus, to consider His beauty, His greatness, His holiness, His majesty, for He is the object of our prayer, as we have seen. Whenever we pray in contemplation it should always be to reflect upon God in the light of Jesus Christ and His teaching. Whenever we pray in contemplation, it should always be to reflect upon the kingdom of God in the light of Jesus Christ and His teaching. And whenever we pray in contemplation, reflecting upon our next life-changing course of action, we should always do so in the light of Jesus Christ and His teaching in seeking the path that God desires us to take. This is the way of true Christian contemplation.

Returning to dictionary definitions for one moment, it will be noticed I am sure, that all of the verbs are *active,* not passive. The Kindle dictionary says of *contemplation*: it is *the action of looking thoughtfully*; the Collins: *to think intently*; the Oxford: *to survey intently, visually or mentally*; and Webster's: *to have in view*. This suggests that contemplative prayer is an *active* means of prayer. This may be a surprise to some readers, for there are those in certain quarters who regard contemplative prayer as being passive, not active. Nevertheless, contemplative prayer is active, for the mind is actively engaged in worshipping, adoring and focusing upon the perceived beauty of Christ (beholding). The worship I'm speaking of is *quiet* worship and adoration of the *heart* and not the *vocalised* worship through *song.*

We have already touched briefly upon the key difference between Christian meditation and Christian contemplation, but it is worth repeating. Christian meditation is prayerful, reflective and objective thought upon the Scriptures. Meditation exploits the power of God's Word. By contrast, Christian contemplation is deep, reflective thought upon Jesus Christ Himself... the action of worshipfully and thoughtfully, reflecting upon Him for a period of time. Christian contemplation, therefore, exploits the power of the person of Jesus Christ. Personal change may be wrought through both meditation and contemplation.

The key differences between contemplative prayer and other forms of Christian prayer are in attention (focus of the mind) and in silence. Attention in contemplative prayer is upon the person of Jesus Christ Himself, as we have said, whereas in petition or intercessory types of prayer, attention is to our own needs or to the needs of others. These needs we bring to the attention of God. Silence in contemplative prayer is of the greatest significance. While the predominant feature of contemplation is silence, the predominant feature of other prayer forms is the spoken word with silent periods generally being few and far between.

Requests play a major role in almost every form of prayer, but in contemplative prayer there are no requests. Participants give to God - rather than receive from Him. They give to God their love, adoration and worship (from the heart). They give to God all of their anxieties, habits and misdemeanours, seeking to let them go and release them to Him. They give to God their heart, their soul and their lives. A balanced Christian life is one that will make room for contemplation without neglecting other forms of Christian prayer.

Contemplative prayer, as we will discover, is like no other means of prayer in terms of the reality of God it brings to the human mind. There is a risk therefore of wanting to exclude other forms of prayer, to live exclusively for contemplation. We must not allow ourselves to be overtaken by such a temptation, but rather use every available means of prayer to our advantage or the advantage of others. Contemplative prayer is indeed powerful and life-changing - we cannot overlook it - but we should not allow it to diminish the importance of other types of prayer either.

The Apostle Paul said: *"I beseech you therefore, brethren, by the mercies of God, that you present your bodies a living sacrifice, holy, acceptable to God, which is your reasonable service. And do not be conformed to this world, but be transformed by the renewing of your mind, that you may prove what* is *that good and acceptable and perfect will of God." (Romans 12:1&2)*

These verses declare what lies at the heart of contemplative prayer; they reveal to us its purpose and its motive. Its purpose is transformation by the renewing of the mind; its motive is surrender to God of everything - in order to know Him in a deeper and more meaningful way.

You may ask the question, "How then does *renewing of the mind* work with regard to purpose?" The way it works is as follows. In silent prayer our attention (focus of the mind) is fixed or centred upon Jesus Christ, whilst at the same time, the heart is actively letting go and releasing to God the negatives: evil thoughts, fears, bad habits, anxieties and sins in order to welcome the positives: His grace, love, goodness, mercies, and presence. Seen in this light, contemplative prayer is essentially an act of repentance. Repentance, as we have seen, is a change of mind leading to a change of direction or a change in habit. Thus, with our attention stayed upon Christ and gradually bringing our thought patterns in line with the will of God, we *are* renewing the mind.

Contemplative prayer then, has a life-changing purpose. However, we must not expect renewal to be achieved overnight. It might happen that quickly of course, since all things are possible with God, but it's more likely that renewal of the mind will be a slower process. It begins *quietly* in the mind and gradually permeates the whole of our being and its fruit manifests itself in our actions.

You may say, "What then, with regard to motive, is meant by surrender to God in order to know Him in

Where Heaven Touches Earth

a deeper and more meaningful way?" Contemplative prayer is also an act of worship, incorporating an act of submission and surrender to God, as we have seen from Romans 12:1, *".... that you present your bodies a living sacrifice, holy, acceptable to God, which is your reasonable service."* Persons engaged in contemplative prayer therefore seek to present every aspect of their lives, both good and bad, to God.

Participants come before God just as they are, without pretence. "Is your life a mess?" "Is your life falling apart?" Then come just as you are; come without any thought of your own personal goodness (or 'badness'), without a praiseworthy list, without airs or graces, without religion, without a holy voice, without request and without a single plea, except that Christ be mediator, your all-in-all *"For there is one God and one mediator between God and men, the Man Christ Jesus" (1Timothy 2:5)*. In this way, participants in contemplative prayer come before God empty (but not in mind), seeking not to be conformed to this world but rather to be transformed by the renewing of their minds. Isaiah said, *"You will guard him and keep him in perfect and constant peace whose mind [both its inclination and its character] is stayed on You, because he commits himself to You, leans on You, and hopes confidently in You." (Isaiah 26:3. The Amplified Bible)* Contemplative prayer, therefore, has a powerful motive.

I'll be bold and ask, "How often in your lifetime can it be said that your mind has been *stayed* on God?" That's a question worth pondering seriously. On a personal note; I've been a Christian for well over forty years and I have to admit there haven't been too many times when I've been conscious of my mind being *stayed* on God, even though I've longed to be in that state and I've longed to know Him on a deeper level. It is my guess that many of us wrestle with the same issues. Contemplative prayer is a simple, uncomplicated way of ensuring that a *mind stayed on God* becomes a living reality... in the process of time.

The Apostle Paul taught us: *"... whatever is true, whatever is worthy of reverence and is honourable and seemly, whatever is just, whatever is pure, whatever is lovely and loveable, whatever is kind and winsome and gracious, if there is any virtue and excellence, if there is anything worthy of praise, think on and weigh and take account of these things [fix your minds on them]." (Philippians 4:8. The Amplified Bible).*

Through contemplative prayer each and every believer has the opportunity to fix their mind on God, learn to abide in His presence and learn to remain in constant communion with Him while engaged in normal everyday activities. You might say to me, "That's a big claim!" Admittedly, to fix one's mind on God is not easy but it can be achieved, believe me, if only for the duration of our contemplation. Again, learning to abide in God's presence is not easy, nor is it easy to remain in constant communion with Him. However, it is possible to fix one's mind, abide in His presence and remain in communion with Him during contemplative prayer. This is but a beginning. In time, we will learn to take these moments of God-consciousness into our everyday experience. By presenting ourselves to God in acts of surrender and giving our love to Him in worship and adoration, we create a 'personal space' where we learn to rest in Him and move beyond life's anxieties and stresses.

This is the way in which the active renewing of the mind works, and the way in which I would define contemplative prayer.

Father God, as I pause to contemplate what has been said and as I take these things in, open my eyes to the real truth and close my eyes to the clever teachings of men who might lead me astray. As the Apostle Paul warned us, "That we henceforth be no more children tossed to and fro, and carried about with every wind of doctrine, by the sleight of men, and cunning craftiness, whereby they lie in wait to deceive." (Ephesians 4:14 AV) Help me to co-operate with the Holy Spirit and put into practice that which will lead me closer to You. In Jesus' name I ask, Amen. (Prayer written by Rob Giles 2014)

10

Contemplative Prayer: The Biblical Basis

"Be still, and know that I am God..." (Psalm 46:10). "... Meditate within your heart on your bed, and be still. Selah" (Psalm 4:4).

Contemplative prayer today is perceived to be somehow shrouded in a mystical cloak of stillness and quiet, and viewed with suspicion. We might ask, "Why is that?" Stillness and quiet are actually powerful tools, but most of us haven't truly recognised them as such, nor have we considered *exploiting* their use. The Psalmist tells us, *"Be still, and know that I am God..." (Psalm 46:10)* This verse gives us every reason to believe that being still is a means of opening a way to knowing God more intimately. Isaiah said, *"...In quietness and confidence shall be your strength..." (Isaiah 30:15)*. This verse tells us that a Christian's strength lies in personal quietness and in personal confidence (faith, trust) in God.

A further reason why contemplative prayer is rarely taught in churches today, and regarded in some quarters as vaguely 'mystical', is that it is deemed to be irrelevant by modern standards, not current, not 'cool' and not masculine. However, by dismissing and casting aside the simple concepts of stillness and quiet, we are in fact closing the door to a wonderful aspect of worship, of strength and of knowing God intimately. We are missing out too on experiencing these hitherto untouched biblical exercises: beholding, watching, waiting and heart-to-heart communing with God.

We may ask the question, "What then is the biblical basis of contemplative prayer?" Psalm 4:4 perfectly describes contemplative prayer: *"...Meditate within your heart on your bed, and be still. Selah"*. To understand this verse, let's break it down.

'Meditate within your heart'.... this means *fixing* your mind on Christ – concentrating solely on Him.

'On your bed'... in the Bible the *bed* often implies rest. So calm down, be quiet and be at rest.

'And be still'... as we have seen from Psalm 46:10, stillness is a means of knowing God more intimately, and if we had any doubts to this point regarding contemplative prayer, the word

'Selah' literally means 'pause to contemplate'.

The Hebrew word for *'be still'*, in Psalm 4:4, is *'damam'*, phonetically pronounced *daw-mam,* and according to Strong's word profiles it means:

"be still, be quiet, be silent, stand still, hold your peace, be struck dumb, be cut down, to cease, to die (destroy)..." [10]

This definition of 'damam' reveals to us what contemplative prayer is really all about. The great exponents of contemplative prayer such as St John of the Cross, Teresa of Avila, Michael Molinos and Jeanne Guyon, to name but a few, taught these things regarding contemplative prayer. Now, however, we see their teaching fulfilled in one biblical Hebrew word - *damam*.

What follows is my interpretation of Strong's definition of that word. I also reflect on Psalm 131 which I consider to be the psalm of contemplation.

The first three injunctions of that definition, *'be still, be quiet, be silent'* I regard as the dynamics of contemplative prayer. Jeanne Guyon said, *"...silence has a great deal to do with experiencing the Lord on a deeper plane."* [11]

Contemplative prayer exploits the powerful dynamics of silence, quiet and stillness in order to know God intimately, a concept perhaps alien to the natural mind. For silence, quiet and stillness are not normally considered to be powerful or dynamic, nor are they considered qualities to be prayerfully exploited for worship or personal advantage.

The next three directives are, *'stand still, hold your peace, be struck dumb'*. These are reflected in both our 'letting go', and in our 'awe of beholding' the breathtaking beauty of Christ. Stand still, hold your peace, be struck dumb i.e. stop what you're doing, say nothing just let go and stand in awe of Christ.

When the children of Israel escaped from Egypt and came to the Red Sea they found themselves trapped... the sea before them, mountains either side of them and the Egyptian army behind them. Moses said to the people, *"...Do not be afraid, stand still* (damam)*, and see the salvation of the Lord, which He will accomplish for you today... The Lord will fight for you, and you shall hold your peace* (damam)." *(Exodus 14:13&14)*

John, on the Isle of Patmos, was awestruck when

he saw the resurrected Christ. He too stood still momentarily and was speechless *(struck dumb)*, and fell like a dead man at the feet of Christ. *(see Revelation 1:17)* We may or may not see the Lord in a vision, but all of us may recognise the majesty of Jesus Christ reflected in the everyday things He does in our lives... if we choose to see them, that is.

Psalm 131 begins by saying, *"Lord, my heart is not haughty, nor my eyes lofty..." (Psalm 131:1)* These attitudes of pride, the *haughty heart* and the *lofty eyes*, are set aside and released to God. There are no places for self-seeking, vainglory or any aspect of pride in the presence of the Lord... so we lay them down and if possible expel them completely from our lives and from 'contemplative prayer'.

The following bid in Strong's definition, *'Be cut down'* – takes attitudes of heart one step further, and also a step deeper. Psalm 131:1 continues by saying, *"...Neither do I concern myself with great matters, nor with things too profound for me."* The *great matters* and the *things too profound* are the cares, concerns and worries of this life. These too are among the things that must be laid down, released and given to God. Those who practise contemplative prayer and want to see it work, seek to release every disturbance within their spirits in order to be still and to be at rest in the presence of the Almighty.

Jesus said *"... do not worry about your life, what you will eat or what you will drink; nor about your body, what you will put on. Is not life more than food and the body more than clothing?"(Matthew 6:25)"*. The New Testament Greek word for 'worry' is *merizo*. Strong says of *merizo*:

"The word suggests a distraction, a preoccupation with things causing anxiety, stress and pressure." [12]

These *distractions* and *preoccupations* are also things that are *'too profound'*. Therefore, the worries, concerns and anxieties of this life are laid down, set aside, in order to embrace the love and companionship of Jesus Christ in the *present* through simple faith in God. These *'great matters'* and *'things too profound'* are found in *tomorrow*, not in today, and as such, should not be our concern. Jesus said, *"...do not worry about tomorrow, for tomorrow will worry about its own things. Sufficient for the day is its own trouble."* (Matthew 6:34) Psalm 131:2 continues by saying, *"Surely I have calmed and quieted my soul..."* in other words, surely I have been *'cut down'*, by not allowing myself to be disturbed and distracted by tomorrow.

Incidentally, the Hebrew word that is translated *'quieted'* in Psalm 131:2 is also the Hebrew word *'damam'*.

The remaining parts of Strong's definition of *damam* are: *'to cease, to die (destroy)'*. This is what Christianity calls 'dying to self'; it is what Paul meant when he said: *"....I die daily."* (1 Corinthians 15:31) Paul also said, *"I have been crucified with Christ; it is no longer I who live, but Christ lives in me; and the life which I now live in the flesh I live by faith in the Son of God, who loved me and gave Himself for me."* (Galatians 2:20) When Paul said, *'I have been crucified with Christ'* he was saying, I have *died* with Christ. When he said, *'it is no longer I who live'*, he was saying 'I have *ceased'* - *ceased* to strive, *ceased* being in my own strength, and *ceased* from my own labours; I trust all of my works and labours to God. The ancient exponents of contemplative prayer, however, speak of God 'destroying the works of the flesh', a concept that is perhaps on the outside of today's thinking although in keeping with the definition of *damam*.

What then is the biblical principle of dying to self? It is basically this: being changed, daily, into the image of Christ, from one degree of glory to another. You might ask, "Do you lose your identity?" Certainly not! We do not lose our identity or our personality, but the image of Christ shines through both. Dying to self is not a one-off transaction but a life-long process. In its simplicity, the process begins with presenting ourselves to God and continues by surrendering, little by little, every aspect of our lives to Him, giving Him our love and trusting our lives to Him on a daily basis. Whilst simple in concept, this may be seen as a mammoth task by many, but its apparent magnitude may be greatly reduced through contemplative prayer.

The act of surrender is not a one-off transaction either; it too is performed on a daily basis. Paul said "....I die daily". And as Psalm 131:2 continues, *"Surely I have calmed and quieted my soul, like a weaned child with his mother; like a weaned child is my soul within me." (Psalm 131:2)* It is, of course, the Holy Spirit who will take us deeper into God. And it is the Holy Spirit who, *like a mother*, will gradually *wean* our soul from fleshly desires including wrong thoughts, bad habits, fears and anxieties. And if you, like me, would like to see changes of this significance take place in your life, then contemplative prayer may be the way forward for you.

Lord Jesus: Change my life and lead me to intimacy, communion, and heart-to-heart fellowship with God so that I may, with all my heart, honour You in all my dealings and bring glory to Your name. Amen. (Prayer written by Rob Giles 2014)

11

Contemplative Prayer: The How?

"My soul, wait silently for God alone, for my expectation is from Him." (Psalm 62:5) "But those who wait on the Lord shall renew their strength; they shall mount up with wings like eagles, they shall run and not be weary, they shall walk and not faint." (Isaiah 40:31)

Contemplative prayer, in its simplest form, is a means of prayer that may be defined as seeking God for who He is, rather than for what we might obtain from Him. It can be said that Christ *Himself* is the object; *silence* is the path; and *intimacy* with God, the goal. You may ask, "How then do we actually do it?" I can only speak from my own experience, so this is my approach…

First I set aside a quiet time and I choose a quiet place. In reality, contemplative prayer may be practised anywhere, at any time and in any situation because the silence we seek is *within* and does not depend upon outward circumstances. But that will take time and much practice to accomplish, so it is easier to begin by finding a quiet and peaceful place in order to concentrate upon achieving the inner quiet and calm, without striving and without wrestling with outside distractions.

We have been advised by many famous preachers that early mornings are a good time to pray. There is an element of truth in this, for there are no activities and few distracting noises. Early mornings worked perfectly for me, while I was labouring in my secular employment. Now, however, due to the medication I am taking (to help me to sleep at night), early mornings are no longer a viable daily option for me. This has led me to believe that we should not feel under pressure to use this particular time of day, for all of us are different. Not everyone is an 'early-bird' and so you may find it more convenient to set aside time last thing at night or some other time of day. The objective is to choose a time and place where it is quiet and you are least likely to be disturbed. Do not berate yourself over the fact that you cannot rise in the small hours and don't feel proud if you can!

Sitting is probably the best position, as it is important to be comfortable and relaxed otherwise the whole *exercise* will be defeated by being restless. I use the word *exercise* because it conveys the sense that contemplative prayer is not only a practice, but also a discipline. The Collins English Dictionary defines exercise as *'an activity to train the body or mind'*. [13]

Those who practise contemplative prayer *train* both their bodies and their minds. They train their bodies to rest and be still and their minds to focus upon God; they also train their ears (within the depth of their beings) to listen for the *'...still small voice'* of the Lord. *(1Kings 19:12)*

You may recall what was said earlier: "Come before God empty"... by that I mean come with nothing, for all that is required of the believer is a humble heart. Set aside your baggage. Come before Him with no agenda, no chorus, no words of Scripture and no music playing softly in the background. Set these things aside in order to meet purely with the Lord and gaze upon His perceived beauty through the eyes of faith for they are a distraction to concentration. These things are not wrong, for there are times in prayer when the Scriptures are crucial; and there are times when worshipful music, playing softly in the background is appropriate to set the scene or 'tone' the mood... but now is not that time. If you are purposefully setting aside time for quiet contemplative prayer, then do it the contemplative way - in silence.

Now I am certainly not advocating the abandonment of other forms of devotion in favour of contemplation. But I am suggesting we adopt silent, contemplative prayer as a regular discipline.

As you sit and wait in calm and quiet, release to God every disturbance and distraction, trying to concern yourself with as little as possible. The 17th Century mystic Michael Molinos puts it like this:

"The mind is calm in the Divine presence. Everything within you is collected, centered and fixed wholly on Him." [14]

This should be our state of mind when we pray in contemplation. If there is agitation, then release it to God.

Silence is something we are not particularly familiar with. Many of us do not like being in total silence and we do not know how to handle it. For instance, if we are holidaying in the country miles from anywhere, experiencing 'quiet', invariably the TV, radio or hi-fi will be on. Few are able to be alone with their own thoughts in absolute silence and sustain it for any length of time. And one of the most difficult things to contend with is what I call the 'inner noise'.

We are so familiar with noise that when it is taken away and there is nothing but absolute silence - it becomes deafening. I have heard many speakers refer to silence in these terms. I think also of the song by Simon and Garfunkel entitled *'The Sound of Silence'* [15]. It is my view that when Paul Simon penned the lyrics of the song, he wasn't merely coining a clever catchphrase, but emphasising a curious fact of life. David Crowder touched on it too in one of his worship songs [16] he spoke of the inner noise. This inner noise, of which I am speaking, is the sound that resonates within when we are in a place of absolute stillness and silence. It occurs because we have never made any attempt to exploit the God-given faculty – *the faculty of silence. "Be still, and know that I am God…" (Psalm 46:10)* I have chosen the term 'faculty' deliberately here. One dictionary definition of 'faculty' is:

"An inherent power or ability; it is any of the powers or capacities possessed by the human mind and it is the ability to perform an act". [17]

I believe inner silence is just such a power.

Silent prayer is not easy. Regularly the mind will become distracted and wander. However, distractions are more likely to come from *within* rather than from without, if you have selected the appropriate time of day. The initial distracting thought will probably be along these lines: "I have to do something, get things going, say something, ask something, anything....!"

But no – just remain in silence and continue giving Jesus Christ your love. It sounds overly simplistic and perhaps a little patronising, but our *ego* is the only thing likely to be bruised in contemplative prayer and, in Christian terms, that is not a particularly bad thing.

We may find that our mind will go off at a tangent, somewhat out of control. It will wander all over the place and we will have great difficulty in controlling our thoughts, staying focused and centred upon Christ. We will be thinking of things like, "What shall I cook for tea?" "I wonder if our team will win tonight." or "I think I'll take a different route to work today." This is the point where many will declare, "Contemplative prayer is not for me!" and give up. But we should not be unduly disturbed or concerned about the wandering of our mind; it is a normal occurrence in these circumstances.

You may say to me, "Aren't we being disrespectful to God when our minds wander?" No, I think not. Children will fall many, many times while learning to walk but no loving parents would ever berate or chastise their children for falling over; they encourage them. Walking is a skill that has to be learnt.

In this respect contemplative prayer is like learning to walk. By attempting to practise contemplative prayer we are learning a new skill. It is a new discipline that will take time to absorb. When our mind wanders, all we need do is gently collect our thoughts and re-centre them once more upon Christ.

Let me put it another way using a very practical example. Imagine yourself seated by a river with a friend, chatting and enjoying each other's company. There's a blue flash and a splash, you turn. 'Wow, did you see that? …a kingfisher.' You return your attention to your friend, 'Where were we...?' and you pick up where you left off. These kinds of distractions often occur, but the interruption doesn't matter to your friend because your relationship is relaxed and secure. It might be regarded as impolite or inappropriate in a different setting – for example in conversation with someone you don't know or in a formal meeting or interview. But life is full of distractions and that momentary interruption will certainly not ruin your relationship with your friend when the bond of friendship is so strong.

Contemplative prayer is about friendship. Sadly, friendship with God appears to be alien to many Christians but it need not be. Jesus said, *"No longer do I call you servants, for a servant does not know what his master is doing; but I have called you friends, for all things that I heard from My Father I have made known to you."* *(John 15:15)* We must not lose sight of His Lordship or of our servanthood, for they are important factors of the Christian life. We will need a *servanthood* approach to God in other forms of prayer and in other aspects of our lives. Contemplative prayer, however, is not characterized by servanthood - it is characterized by friendship. It is not ritual - it is relationship. It is not conversation - it is communion. How else could the Apostle John get away with leaning on Christ's bosom (chest) at the last supper? Or how else could Mary get away with sitting at Christ's feet while her sister served? It was friendship with Christ, pure and simple; it was relationship and it was communion. If we are able to capture this concept, it will be an invaluable lesson to learn in our journey to intimacy with God… made easier through contemplative prayer.

To practise silent prayer persistently, half-an-hour per day for a few months will change your life considerably. But you will have to stick with it. It is rather like taking a course of antibiotics. We all know that we're unlikely to feel any benefit from the first, second, third or even the fourth tablet or capsule. We have to persist with them and complete the prescribed course. The same is true with contemplative prayer... except the prescribed course is a lifetime! Once you've begun, you must stick with it on a daily basis. If you don't, what you have gained through contemplation will very soon slip away and be lost. The reality of God can be so authentic at times but, like life itself, at other times so very, very flimsy. But it is easily regained for God is often closer than we think.

The more we are able to let go and release our inner hold on confusion, anxiety, wayward thoughts and cares of the heart, the better, for we will be releasing them to God and actively looking to Him to replace them with His love and presence. In time, their grip will weaken and our love for God will grow stronger. *"We love Him because He first loved us." (1John 4:19)*

We may discover, to our amazement, that silent prayer will lead us to a *rest* we once thought unachievable. As the writer to the Hebrews says *"There remains therefore a rest for the people of God. For he who has entered His rest has himself also ceased from his works as God did from His." (Hebrews 4:9&10)*

The prophet Isaiah said these remarkable words and they most certainly apply to contemplative prayer: *"He gives power to the weak, and to those who have no might he increases strength. Even the youths shall faint and be weary, and the young men shall utterly fall, but those who wait on the Lord shall renew their strength; they shall mount up with wings like eagles, they shall run and not be weary, they shall walk and not faint." (Isaiah 40: 29–31)*

The Scripture tells us those who *wait… shall…*; this is an awesome promise that has the potential of becoming an even greater reality. God is faithful to His promises, God is faithful to Himself, God is faithful to his love and God is faithful to His presence. Instead of searching outwardly in frustration for God, why not look inwardly…in silence? To your astonishment you may find Him there… in the most unlikely of places.

Lord, as I sit in Your presence and reach out to You from the depth of my being, please reach out to me. Open my heart and grant the quiet confidence to believe that You are with me, never to leave me and never to forsake me. Amen. (Prayer written by Rob Giles 2014)

12

Contemplative Prayer: Quietude

"...That you put off, concerning your former conduct, the old man which grows corrupt according to the deceitful lusts, and be renewed in the spirit of your mind, and that you put on the new man which was created according to God, in true righteousness and holiness." (Ephesians 4:22-24)

It has long been accepted that *'mood'* can affect physical health and wellbeing. The Bible supports this view by saying: *"A merry heart does good, like medicine, but a broken spirit dries the bones." (Proverbs 17:22)*. If you are able to raise your mood, it can be a very effective means of raising levels of serotonin in the brain.

Serotonin is a monoamine neurotransmitter, generally associated with happiness and well being. We are told that increases in brain serotonin can help to protect against the onset of depression.

In an article published in the Journal of Psychiatry & Neuroscience, dated November 2007, Simon N. Young discussed non-pharmacological (without drugs) methods of raising levels of serotonin in the brain. [18] Young suggests that mood and serotonin work both ways, mood affecting serotonin and serotonin affecting mood.

In the article, Young discusses four strategies for raising serotonin without medication. One of which is of particular interest in the light of what we have been discussing in the previous three chapters… and that is changes in thought.

It's not a new concept that alterations in brain serotonin can be brought about by psychotherapy. Nor is it new that alterations in brain serotonin can be brought about by self induced changes in thought. However, I found it very surprising to discover that increases in the neurotransmitter dopamine can be brought about through meditation. [19] (Dopamine is the neurotransmitter that helps control the brain's reward and pleasure centres). Christian leaders have been telling us for years that meditating upon the Scriptures (the Word of God) can lift our mood and lift our spirits. Here, however, we have scientific support that meditation can stimulate mood.

Participants of Christian contemplative prayer, as I have said elsewhere, are actively seeking to change their thinking in order to cooperate with God in the renewal of the mind. Through personal experience, I can confirm that Christian contemplative prayer can lift our mood in the same way that Christian meditation can.

On a personal note, as I have previously stated, I went through a difficult time when I had a mental and emotional breakdown. I suffered from deep depression at that time and I was overwhelmed by my struggle with alcohol (each affecting the other). Every day I was *tortured* by anxiety. And those who have suffered from anxiety will know that it can be very torturous.

I felt that anxiety was slowly eating me away and keeping me on the edge of what seemed like a precipice. I was very conscious of my personal fears and uncertainties and as a result I was stressed to the hilt. My mood was up and down, rarely stable. *My* 'ups' were manic and *my* 'downs' depressive. This was my mental state prior to discovering contemplative prayer. I shall say more on this experience in a subsequent chapter.

I had a sleep disorder and I'd often wake in the small hours 3.00 or 4.00 a.m. sometimes as early as 1.00 a.m. Once awake, I could not fall asleep again. I began to turn those sleepless spells into periods of silent prayer and adoration. I would tiptoe down stairs and sit in silence, with the lights off and focus my being upon Jesus Christ in my broken state of mind. As I sat and waited on God in silent contemplation, I tried to fill my mind with thoughts of Christ and of God. As I did so, many Scriptures flowed through my mind expanding my comprehension and understanding of Jesus Christ. This is Christian meditation, where one meditates upon the Word of God.

It was the silence and apparent *nothingness* of contemplative prayer that led me into meditation upon the Scriptures. At that particular time I didn't possess the mental prowess to launch straight into meditating upon God's Word. This is one reason why I believe that Christian contemplation in its simplest and purest form is a gift from God to the broken mind. It is such, that it can lead the broken mind into other forms of prayer and take the damaged soul on a journey into rest. As Jesus said himself, *"Come to Me, all of you who labor and are heavy laden, and I will give you rest. Take my yoke upon you and learn from Me, for I am gentle and lowly in heart and you will find rest to your souls."* Matthew 11:28 & 29

I sought, further, in my silent prayer times, to remain as *still* and as quiet as I could inside. And as much as was possible throughout the rest of my day, I sought to stay *still* and think on Christ. As often as I could, I would talk with Him while I worked. Anything that gave me the slightest disturbance arousing fear or anxiety, I would release it to God. This 'releasing to God' was not a one off transaction. I performed this mental and emotional exercise over and over throughout each day. These things are worth pursuing. I think that both Christian contemplation and meditation are great news for the Christian who suffers from time to time with depression.

Now at that particular time I did not know that what I was doing was contemplative prayer. Nor did I have any grasp of what was taking place because I was in a broken state of mind and simply trying to survive from one day to the next. It was only later that I realised my mind was slowly being renewed by God. All I had done was simply create a space (in silence) to allow God to work on my behalf. My mood began to change. I saw many changes take place in a very short space of time. There were fewer ecstatic highs and fewer depressive lows. Somehow, miraculously, I became aware that I was gradually living on a much more level plane than ever before.

It was in the summer of 2012 that I discovered, on

the internet, the above article by Simon N. Young. I went cold as I read it – I was speechless. I had, in point of fact, come through - and come out of deep depression *without* medication. This was *my* experience. I am not advocating that anyone should attempt the same. Medication for many people is right and appropriate way forward. I had simply followed the advice the Lord Jesus Christ had given to me in the visitations. The parallels with Young's article were quite extraordinary to me.

There is a great deal to be said for being quiet. When we are quiet we are much more receptive to the voice of the Holy Spirit, because we are attentive and listening. It is much easier for the Holy Spirit to reveal to us the hidden secrets of our heart, simply because we have no agenda and no 'shopping list' type of prayers. I'm not saying that we *have* to be quiet in order to listen, for God has many ways of getting our attention. But when we are intentionally and purposefully setting aside a specific time to listen, we are putting ourselves in *God's way*, attentive and expectant and waiting for Him to speak.

What we must beware of is *deliberately* keeping ourselves busy so as not to hear His voice. Such behaviour only shows, subconsciously, we are fearful of what we might discover about ourselves. In truth, God does not reveal the secrets of our hearts to condemn us; He only reveals them to fashion us into the image of His Son, the Lord Jesus Christ.

Over time, practising contemplative prayer will indeed change our attitude. You don't need a supernatural visitation like what happened to me. Practising contemplative prayer will help all of us

Where Heaven Touches Earth

to deal with emotional and mental anguish in an appropriate manner.

For example: What if a close friend hurts us with unkind words? How do we deal with the emotional hurt we feel? Of course we have to talk to our friend and try to bring about reconciliation, but that aside… how do we deal with the mental and emotional hurt we feel?

To deal with this hurt, we can follow the path of contemplation. The do's and don'ts are these. First and foremost, *do not* react. Secondly, *do not* chew it over in your mind. Thirdly, *do* find somewhere quiet to be silent and alone with God. *Do* come to Christ as a friend and imagine that He is there with you, not so much as Lord but as your friend. *Do* tell Him that you love Him and thank Him for His nearness. *Do* tell how you feel and that you're not sure if you are handling the hurt in the appropriate 'God way'. Then be silent… visualise the hurt and then visualise your giving it to Him. Follow this procedure of releasing to God as often as you can. Repeatedly giving and releasing to Him. This is the key that will unlock 'the Christ' within you.

I was amazed the first time I tried it for myself. Formerly, I would have carried my hurt around for several months whilst attempting to come to terms with what my friend had done. But to my astonishment the sting of pain had gone within a day or so. I was then able to think the whole event through rationally to a positive conclusion. You might ask, "Why is that?" The reason is this - my judgements were no longer clouded by my hurt.

Make no mistake about it; quiet, silence, letting go and releasing to God are powerful tools. Do not underestimate their power. Let us take what we have learnt about contemplation and put it to use, for we will discover that the path of contemplation will help us when we meet some of life's most difficult of challenges.

The greatest of life's challenges I think is death. I'm not thinking particularly of our own death, but the death of someone around us. The death of a loved one, for instance, a family member, a close friend, a colleague or a neighbour, each of us will have to face such an event at least once if not several times in our lifetime. Contemplation will be a great asset for the reasons I have already given: "quiet, silence, letting go and releasing to God are powerful tools. Do not underestimate their power."

The greatest benefit any Christian can have is that of God's abiding presence. This is the prize, the goal that all Christians who long to know God more intimately are pressing toward. Contemplative prayer is a simple, uncomplicated means of pressing towards that goal. For some reason or another, contemplative prayer stimulates faith and makes the heart more receptive to the Holy Spirit. Some might ask, "Why?" I cannot give a definitive answer, but the best reason I can come up with is simply this - in contemplative prayer the heart seeks to remain lowly and lowliness is a great quality to possess. Lowliness is one of the very few 'rules' of contemplation (that's if you can call it a rule - perhaps 'imperative' may be a better term). Let us therefore welcome lowliness - let us embrace lowliness and take it to our heart.

God is with us, in our corner, in our pain, in our sorrow, in our grief, in our heartache, in our mess, in our world. Heaven is reaching down to touch *our* earth.

Let us quietly and calmly reach out and take hold of that providence. And may our lives become a *chalice* into which Christ may pour the wine of His love, joy and peace.

Heavenly Father, I thank You for Your Son, who is at work in our lives to change us by the power of the Holy Spirit. Help me to co-operate with You and with Your Word. Help me to 'create the space' for You to renew my mind and transform my life, in Jesus' name, Amen. (Prayer written by Rob Giles 2014)

13

A Question of Death

"For the living know that they will die..." (Ecclesiastes 9:5) He will swallow up death forever, and the Lord God will wipe away tears from all faces... (Isaiah 25:8)

We now come face to face with what is arguably one of life's most difficult challenges – the death of a loved one - for there is only one thing absolutely certain in life and that is death. All of us are aware that death is inevitable, but we choose not to think about it most of the time. In adolescence, death appears to be a lifetime away and is therefore the last thing on our minds.

When we are young we tend to associate death with old age, but of course, there is no certainty that any of us will ever reach old age. When we hear on the news of children dying from cancer or being hit by a car outside school or a young person taking their own life, it brings us down to earth with a bump. Should we be fortunate enough to reach old age, we only too readily realise that the years have flown by. For some unknown reason, the time of leaving school and our teenage years are still vivid memories, yet we may have difficulty remembering what we did yesterday.

All of us will respond differently to the death of family members, friends or someone special. No matter how philosophical or stoical our stance on life, an untimely death can move us from our place of calm and rationality. There is no way of knowing how we might behave in the event of a sudden death.

On a personal note: On the 4th of February 1966, just two months prior to my leaving school, my cousin John took his own life. This event had a profound effect upon me as an impressionable fifteen year-old. Nothing could have prepared me for such a tragedy. It shook the family to the core. The stance of the Church in general in those days and the stigma attached to suicide was soul-destroying. The immediate family never got over it and John's parents carried their heartache, grief and guilt with them to the grave. I say 'guilt' because families do take upon themselves an enormous amount of guilt and feel in some way responsible, whether justifiable or not. "If only..." "If only I'd done this or that..." "If only I'd said this or that..." "What if... What if..." Suicide has a vile way of transmitting and transferring guilt upon those who are left behind.

A few months later, after leaving school, a girl I had been trying to date from my old form died suddenly from pneumonia. I had fancied this girl right from my first day at secondary school. I have to admit that it cut me up. I was inconsolable. I broke down and I cried rivers of tears. Most likely the grief I felt was compounded by my cousin's tragic death; nevertheless, it did have a deep impact upon me. I still think about her from time to time, even though I have been happily married for over forty years. There is no way of knowing how any of us might react to an untimely death, even more so if the event is compounded by additional problems.

The way in which we react could depend upon several factors: our attachment to the deceased, our mood at the time, the circumstances of the death or even the situation we find ourselves in. We may have recently lost our job, been going through a break-up or divorce, been in financial difficulty, faced the prospect of losing our home or a whole host of reasons that will have a major impact upon our lives and have a dramatic effect upon our response to an untimely death.

There is never a 'good' time for a loved one to die, but sometimes the timing can be absolutely abysmal, scupper our plans, or bring to an end a golden opportunity. Such as a daughter having the chance to go to university... the father dies suddenly and the daughter has to drop out and look after her sick or broken-hearted mother. Or a son who has the opportunity to take a year out and work amongst refugees in some far-flung corner of the globe. The father dies suddenly and the son has to take over the management of the family business. These things sometimes happen in life and when they do, it can feel so very, very cruel. Such shocks can and do rock our world. Undeniably they have the potential to shape us for the rest of our lives, for better or worse, if we allow them to.

When someone close to us dies, it can be a mixed bag, a rollercoaster of emotions. The Bible uses phrases such as: *"the sorrows of death" (Psalm 18:4 AV)*, *"the snares of death" (Psalm 18:5 AV), "the valley of the shadow of death" (Psalm 23:4 AV), "the terrors of death" (Psalm 55:4 AV), "the pangs of death" (Psalm 73:4 AV)* and *"the bitterness of death" (Ecclesiastes 7:26 AV).* Those who have lost someone dear may recognise these phrases to be true in their experience.

Again on a personal note, I recall my 28th birthday. My mother died suddenly two days before, and was buried three days after my birthday. Some might say, "That must have been a rubbish birthday, and I bet no birthday was ever the same after that!" It certainly was a rubbish birthday and it did indeed pass me by, but I didn't allow my mother's death to rob me of enjoying other birthdays. I stopped and thought about it, and reasoned with myself that my mother would not have wanted her death to stop me enjoying the rest of my life. I also had a lovely wife and four small children to whom I was responsible. I chose to take my responsibility seriously rather than be overcome by misery. My reasoning to find a way through my grief, gave me an amazing opportunity to support my father and teenage brother during that first year following her death.

With regard to my feelings towards my mother's death, there was no guilt on my part. I have fond memories of her and I foster and cherish those memories. I know I'll never forget her. She was a Christian and I know that one day I will see her again. Given another time or a different set of circumstances, however, I might well have reacted differently. And yes, possibly I would have ended up hating birthdays for the rest of my life.

I will say it again - there is no way of knowing how

we might respond to an untimely death. Sadly, there is no way of preparing for such an event either. Even if our loved one is terminally ill and we know that death is imminent, it is still a blow when it takes place.

Over the years many have derived comfort from poetry and a short piece of prose, such as, 'Death is nothing at all' [23] and 'What is dying?' [24]

These pieces are often read at funerals. They may be found on certain sympathy cards, bookmarks and plaques which maybe purchased at any Christian bookshop.

Heaven is 'nearer' than we think and Jesus Christ is willing to step into our grief, our heartache and our pain if only we will allow him.

Of course we may never get over the death of someone we love dearly and I'm not suggesting that we do, but we can in some measure come to terms with that loss. We can work through our grief as we will see from the following story, a classic example of heaven touching earth. We will witness how God stepped into the lives of Clive and Sylvia (both as a couple and individually) when one of their young daughters was tragically killed in a road traffic accident.

We can work through our grief. We can come to terms with our loss - in some measure. Engage in bereavement counselling if necessary. By every means available to us, we must work through our grief. Don't pooh-pooh the idea of bereavement counselling because it is imperative to find a way through or else we may run the risk of being damaged emotionally.

The mind can and does play tricks with us; our behaviour can be irrational and our thinking illogical. "Oh! I mustn't do this or that." "I must leave things just as she liked them." "I'm not going out to enjoy myself or I'll be letting him down."

The process of coming to terms with tragic loss and adjusting to the gaping hole the loved one has left is difficult. It takes time, of course, and we must do whatever is necessary to encourage ourselves, build faith and move on with the rest of our lives. But we must steer clear of the things that bring us down, because the loss itself is enough to contend with.

Dear Lord, as I walk through this dark period of my life, allow me to sense Your nearness. Speak to my heart as I read Your word or as I read people's inspiring stories. Lord, give me Your peace and keep my life in Your hands. Amen. (Prayer written by Rob Giles 2014)

14

Clive and Sylvia's Story: Surprised by Peace and Love

"He tends His flock like a shepherd: He gathers the lambs in His arms and carries them close to His heart; He gently leads those that have young." (Isaiah 40: 11 NIV)

Whilst on their way to pick up their eight year-old daughter, Alex, from a Church Pastoral Aid Society (CPAS) children's camp in Sidmouth, Devon. Clive and Sylvia's Vauxhall Calibra was involved in a life-changing traffic accident where their four and a half year-old daughter, Holly, was killed. This is their story... They speak frankly about the tragedy and tell how God revealed His loving presence in their shattered world.

Clive was driving their coupe and Sylvia was seated in the passenger seat next to him. Holly was strapped into a child's seat behind Clive and his father was sitting next to Holly. When the incident happened they were travelling along the A35 between Dorchester and Bridport at around 9.15am on a section of road that was more like a cutting through the hillside which had no footpaths. As they were slowly travelling up a hill in a long queue of traffic behind a hay lorry, an out-of-control car appeared over the hill, coming towards them. They watched as it hit the embankment, rolled onto its side and slid towards them. It struck the offside 'quarter light' window of their car, just behind the driver, flipped onto its roof rolling over several times before coming to rest some distance down the road. Unfortunately, Holly had been looking out of that window. She eventually died in hospital at around 1pm from the massive head injury she had sustained.

Commenting on the crash, Clive explained, "There were five people in the wrecked car, four little boys and a woman driver, and all five walked away with only minor cuts and bruises. Our car had a scrape down the side and the small smashed window. Compared to the other vehicle, you would not have thought ours had been involved in a fatal accident. The other car, however, was a different story!"

Clive and Sylvia described Alex and Holly as totally different personalities. "Alex was quiet and rather shy, while Holly was lively, confident and extrovert. They were soul buddies as well as sisters and Holly was Alex's 'confidence'. Holly was simply full of life; she lived her life to the full, always pushing boundaries and trying new things. We always knew that when the girls were up to mischief, Holly would have been the instigator. However, when they were seated quietly doing something like art and craft, the activity would have originated from Alex!"

When asked, "Was there a process you went through

in dealing with grief?" Sylvia replied, "Yes, and there still is. It is very much an ongoing process. There are still times when the whole devastation washes over me, and days when I really struggle. Those days, for me, have got further and further apart but I still have my moments, when I may spend the whole day just missing her."

"People say, don't they, time heals?" Clive interjected "Well actually, no, it doesn't. It doesn't heal! I don't think anything can heal what you've gone through – but time helps. As Sylvia said, the intervals between those hard times just get further apart. It often affects us when we are tired or run down, or on significant dates like Holly's birthday. Milestones, like becoming a teenager, her 18th birthday and 15th December 2011 when it would have been her 21st birthday, have all been particularly poignant. That feels like the last 'milestone' now – we don't feel, for example, that her 30th will affect us in the same way."

"One thing I've learnt about grief," continued Clive, "is that people don't know what to say to you. There was a guy that I got on really well with at work. I was walking down the high street and he just blanked me completely. I turned round and said 'Hi'. He turned and said, 'I'm sorry Clive I didn't know what to say to you.' This part of grief is really difficult because it's you that has to break the ice. Its not that they don't care or that they don't love you, it's just that they genuinely don't know what to say. So I've learnt to talk to grieving people – however difficult that is – because our experience is that to ask grieving people to make the first move is unfair!"

"Some of the key moments for me," said Sylvia,

Where Heaven Touches Earth

"were when God spoke to me. These happened around three weeks after we had moved house because of Clive's job relocation. We were renting accommodation in an area we didn't know. Clive eventually went back to work, Alex started her new school and I was left alone during the day. I was personally hassled by the press at this time due to the nature of the accident. While Clive was at work a large number of them came and knocked on the door with cameras seeking interviews. Of course the grief was at its rawest and raging at the time – and I felt very much alone. We didn't know anyone – we'd only twice visited the Church we eventually made our home. We had no family or Church family close to us to turn to. I was at the lowest point in my life. However, our God of love is there in these times as well. Let me tell you of two really special occasions where He presented Himself."

"The first time was while I was out walking our dog on my own in some woods adjacent to the house. I had been taking comfort and strength from Psalm 23 for several days and found, right in the middle of the wood, two dead but still upright trees – one was in the perfect shape of a shepherd's crook and the other in the perfect shape of a staff. I knew straight away that God was demonstrating Psalm 23 to me right in front of my eyes!"

"The second time God spoke to me was when I was trying to use our new computer for the first time – it was all unfamiliar to me and I could not get my head around this machine! I had bits of paper and the instruction booklet in my hand and I just threw them all up in the air, sobbing and screaming at God, 'I can't do this'; and then it tumbled out... 'I don't want to live anymore!'"

At that moment I knew I was seriously hurting and felt my own words freezing in the air surrounding me. But they were not the only words I was to remember that day. Almost as soon as I had spoken, a response came back at me... 'I love you Sylvia'. It was audible. There was a door behind me and I looked for the source of the voice – but I knew it wasn't that Clive had come home early. I'd never heard it before... and I've never heard it since. But those four words have kept me going, have kept me believing; I *know* He loves me! It was such a privilege to hear the *audible* voice of God. It was a voice that resonated through my body, mind and soul; it was warm, strong and comforting and it has stayed with me. I have always believed and never doubted that there is a God – partly for that reason. He too, is a father who watched His child die; He was as fully present then as He was with me in my agony over 2000 years later."

"Holly's death has changed my life," said Clive. "My life has changed massively in different ways. I wasn't a Christian at the time. If you'd asked me then, I would have said I was. I think I'd always believed there was a God, but I was living two lives. I was living my life at home and my life at work – and they were different. I now understand that I wasn't a Christian, even though I'd been going to Church for over 15 years! We had always gone to Anglican Churches, but all the Churches we'd been to were small and not very 'lively'. However, during the process of house-hunting, and finding an area in which to settle, we visited St Sebastian's."

"We had visited the Church twice before Holly died and even though it was more charismatic than we were used to, for some reason (which we now know!) we felt it was the right one. The vicar, Derek, and the rest of the Church family were amazing. Actually, one of the helpful things Derek said to us very early on, and this has stuck with me, was 'Please don't be too Christian about this'. Actually he was right. As Christians we can put on masks, we can pretend everything is alright – we are Christians after all, and we should be happy! Well, of course you can scream and shout at God! Like a child that can scream and shout at a father, probably about something totally trivial or irrelevant but just releasing feelings, we can do that with God – our Heavenly Father. The Psalms are fantastic for this. They are so helpful. There's no need for us to feel guilty about getting mad and shouting at God. He's big enough to take it."

"Immediately after the accident, both of us had about twenty-four to forty-eight hours of screaming and shouting. All the things you'd expect in terms of anger, whatever... but I'm not sure if anger is the right word actually, certainly screaming and shouting and frustration. However, with trauma like this, one can often assume God isn't there and move away from Him, but for me it was the opposite, I knew He was there, because something happened that I really struggle to describe. There was this... amazing *peace*. I don't mean that I didn't cry, because I did. But we knew where Holly was. We thought, 'If she could go through death – then we certainly could.'"

"A lady from our old Church spoke to us one day and she said that she had been given a picture by God that describes perfectly how it was for us at the time. The picture was of two pillars with a blanket over the top. Sylvia, Alex and I were on top of the blanket with people underneath with their hands held high praying for us. She explained that Jesus had been represented by the two pillars, giving strength and support, whilst the people were praying – lifting us up over the pain – and that was absolutely how it happened in reality. In our pain there was peace. There was pain, and of course we were upset – but there was *Peace!*"

"A few months later, after taking part in an Alpha Course at St Sebastian's, I finally let the Holy Spirit come into my life and I became a Christian – a real Christian! So, amazingly Holly's death had saved me. There is a book that my great, great grandfather wrote in the late eighteen hundreds and he gave this illustration about a boy who wanted to lead the mother sheep to safety. He takes the lamb on his shoulders and the mother follows. There was a picture in the book showing the shepherd taking the lamb and the sheep following. It's a picture that speaks so much to me, because that's what has happened to me. Jesus has Holly on His shoulders and I followed after Him – and that is where I am."

"There are times when I feel myself cry even now 17 years later, but it has changed my outlook on life massively. The fact that I'm a Christian now and I wasn't before is really a big change. I don't think I could say that I could be thankful for it but in an odd way there is an element of that. At the time, I was absorbed in work and when something like that happens it brings you back to earth; it's really what life is all about. I confess that from time to time I slip into that mode and I try to bring myself back out of it… Grief can take you both ways. It can either split you up or bring you together. With us, it brought us together."

"Our peace has continued. There have even been points, we think, when people were saying that Sylvia and Clive were not handling it well. They actually believed that through this tragic scenario we hadn't grieved properly. I can understand that, but they hadn't seen us at home. They hadn't witnessed the tears, the days of devastation we felt from time to time, where it just washed over us – and we missed her so very much. But as strange as this sounds, even though our emotions got the better of us, we still had that peace."

"There is nothing we cannot go through now," said Sylvia, "having gone through that, we can face anything with God. Death has lost its sting. The sovereignty of God is revealed most intimately and magnificently when overcoming the pain of death. Even when things like our marriage go through difficult times, we just know He is going to carry us out to the other side. In our suffering and need, He is, and will always be – Love."

Faithful God, we praise You that You are with us in the highs and You are with us in the lows. You are with us in the good times and with us in the bad times. You are Lord in life and You are Lord in death. Help us to see that the dark times in our lives can be opportunities for you to work on our behalf. We thank You for the help You lend and the strength you give, in the name of Jesus Christ our Lord. Amen. (Prayer written by Rob Giles 2014)

15

A Question of Grief

"For my life is spent in grief, and my years with sighing... (Psalm 31:10) "I am weary of my groaning; all night I make my bed swim; I drench my couch with my tears. My eye wastes away because of grief..." (Psalm 6: 6&7) "And all his sons and all his daughters arose to comfort him; but he refused to be comforted, and he said, 'for I shall go down into the grave to my son in mourning,' Thus his father wept for him." (Genesis 37:35)

Most of us are familiar with the grief surrounding the death of a loved one. We know there is a grieving process as we have seen from Clive and Sylvia's story. That grieving process may be difficult and, more than likely, will be different for each of us. Nevertheless, we have to grieve. We grieve for what we have lost in order to welcome the future we have in store. In grief, many will feel their world has fallen apart or that the emptiness within will swallow them up - that is to be expected. Life at such times can seem unfair, uncertain, unreasonable and so unbelievably painful. I like the way Wikipedia describes grief:

"A multi-faceted response to loss" [22]

The Bible, especially the Old Testament, has much to say about grief. There are many different Hebrew words that are translated *grief* and their meanings collectively reveal to us the multi-faceted nature of grief. For example, Isaiah says of the Messiah: *"...A man of sorrows and acquainted with grief..." (Isaiah 53:3)* And verse 4 of the same passage exclaims, *"Surely he has borne our griefs..."* The Hebrew word translated grief in both cases is *choli* meaning *grief, sickness, weakness and pain.* The Psalmist says, *"For my life is spent with grief, and my years with sighing..." (Psalm 31:10).* The Hebrew word there is *yagon,* and means *grief, sorrow and affliction.* You may recall that Job's friends came to see him when he lost everything. The Scripture says, *"So they sat down with him on the ground seven days and seven nights, and no one spoke a word to him, for they saw that his grief was very great." (Job 2:13)* The Hebrew word here is *keeb,* and means *grief and pain.* In Psalm 6 the Psalmist says, *"I am weary of my groaning; all night I make my bed swim; I drench my couch with my tears. My eye wastes away because of grief..." (Psalm 6: 6&7)* The Hebrew word here is *kaas* and means *grief, sadness, provocation and anger.* Genesis 26:34&35 records, *"When Esau was forty years old, he took as wives Judith the daughter of Beeri the Hittite, and Basemath the daughter of Elon the Hittite. And they were a grief of mind to Isaac and Rebecca."* Grief here is *morah* and means *grief and bitterness.* In 1 Samuel 25:30&31, Abigail said to David, *"And it shall come to pass, when the Lord has done for my lord according to all the good that He has spoken concerning you and has appointed you ruler over Israel, that this will be no grief to you..."* On this occasion the word used is *pugah* and means *grief, a stumbling block*. This is by no means a definitive list, for there are other Hebrew words that are translated as *grief*. But the meanings of these Hebrew words offer a comprehensive definition of the multi-faceted nature of grief i.e. sickness, weakness, pain, sorrow, affliction, sadness, provocation, anger, bitterness and a stumbling block.

Grief is mainly associated with the death of a loved one: spouse, child, father, mother, sister, brother, grandparent, relative, friend or colleague. But there is also what is called *disenfranchised* grief. It is worth being aware of disenfranchised grief because many people experience it without knowing what it is or without realising what is taking place. Disenfranchised grief

Grief, when it is disenfranchised, may be associated with a broken marriage, a miscarriage, an abortion or the surrender of a child for adoption. It can be expressed in times of loss such as the loss of personal health, the loss of a limb or severe disablement, the loss of a home, the loss of a job, or the loss of a pet. It may also be expressed by someone whose loved one is terminally ill or has lost the ability to function properly because of illness, senile dementia, Alzheimer's disease, Motor-neurone disease or Parkinson's disease etc. The sadness, sorrow, anger and bitterness experienced are all aspects of 'disenfranchised grief'. But they *are grief* nevertheless and should be treated as such.

A further example of disenfranchised grief may be the death of a celebrity. Powerful expressions of this were witnessed in the United States at the death of Elvis Presley, and again in the United Kingdom at the death of Diana, Princess of Wales, when virtually the whole nation appeared to mourn and many wept openly in the streets.

Grief may also manifest itself when moving away from familiar surroundings occasioned, perhaps, by a spouse's change of job, or when moving abroad. It may commonly be called 'home sickness' but it is, nevertheless, an expression of grief.

Grief can be compounded by the death of a loved one in socially unacceptable circumstances, such as suicide, drug overdose, alcoholism, AIDS. Loved ones not only experience the grief surrounding the loss of their family member or friend, but also the disenfranchisement often caused by people's dismissive attitude towards that particular type of death. Should the body of the loved one never be recovered, such as in war or murder, grief is compounded still further because the element of closure is taken away.

Grief, itself, may become disenfranchised when well-meaning family or friends seek to put a time limit on your right to grieve. This is where grief becomes a *stumbling block*. Your grief is a stumbling block, inasmuch as it is perceived to be preventing you from returning to so-called 'normality'. But it is also a stumbling block to you, because the unnecessary restrictions being placed upon you have caused disenfranchised grief, additional confusion, heartache and pain. Such a scenario can only prolong the grieving process. You may, at such a time, feel pressed into believing the untruth (or even convince yourself), "I'll never get over this!" ...which is in itself a stumbling block.

Those who experience disenfranchised grief need

to know: "You have the right to grieve." Often those who experience disenfranchised grief are not comforted, affirmed or validated, but they need to be. No one has the right to say that your grief is unacceptable because, regardless of what people say, it is still grief.

Therapist and grief counsellor, Elizabeth Kupferman has much to say about grief and grief when it is disenfranchised, it is worth checking it out. [23]

It is not abnormal to grieve. When you lose someone close it is right and proper to grieve that lose. To resist grief or to fight against it can be damaging. We must accept that grief is a natural response to the death of someone with whom a bond has been forged. It could be a bond of adulation, fondness, respect, friendship or of love. Most of us will understand we will grieve when a bond of friendship or a love has been broken. But let's look briefly at the former three.

Fans form a bond of adulation with their icons, heroes and so on, such as footballers, sport stars, pop stars and film stars etc. When an icon or hero dies that bond of adulation has been severed. This is the reason why fans grieve. It may be called disenfranchised grief but it is grief nevertheless.

The Collins English Dictionary & Thesaurus says of fond.

"Having a liking for" [24] I speak of fondness in this way.

You may be fond of a newsreader or a personality, either male or female it doesn't matter it is someone you like. The bond of fondness is not quite what you would describe as adulation. However, when that person dies the bond of fondness and the liking you have developed no longer exists as it did, therefore you grieve. The sadness you feel though disenfranchised grief is still grief.

To respect someone is to hold them in high regard or to esteem them highly. This is very different to adulation and fondness. You admire that person's integrity or what they stand for. If that person dies that bond is severed and you grieve. I recall the death of the English, Labour Party politician, Tony Benn. There was a massive turnout to his funeral and members of all political parties mourned his passing. The keynote was respect. Whether they agreed or disagreed with his views they admired his integrity and they held him in high esteem. This is one that could be termed both, disenfranchised grief at the loss of someone highly esteemed or genuine grief at the loss of a valued colleague.

In 1969, Elizabeth Kubler-Ross, a psychiatrist and pioneer in near-death studies, introduced what is now known as the five stages of grief. [31] The five stages are based upon her studies regarding the feelings of patients facing terminal illness. Many people over the years, however, have generalized them to other types of negative life changes and losses, such as coming to terms with the death of a loved one, alcohol and drug abuse, sexual abuse, a break-up, divorce or even to the loss of a limb. In simple terms the five stages of grief are: denial, anger, bargaining, depression and acceptance.

The five stages are only a loose framework and are not set in stone. They do, however, give us a guide as to what may be taking place when we meet with life-changing issues and personal loss. What follows is my interpretation of the five stages of grief.

Denial is the initial response to the death of a loved one. Denial is where we find it difficult to believe what is taking place. "This cannot be happening!" As we have seen denial is something that is very real in alcoholism. It is something that is taught in the Twelve Steps programme and AA.

Anger is a natural reaction to the death of a loved one. We may be angry at the loss. We may be angry with the circumstances surrounding the loss. We may be angry with ourselves. We may be angry with someone else if we feel that person is to blame. Or, we may simply be angry with God. Anger is a normal response to the death of a loved one. Alcoholics may be angry with others because they feel that no one understands. They may feel anger with themselves because they cannot stop drinking.

What of bargaining? There will almost invariably be some form of bargaining attached to grief. Or maybe there's some kind of 'deal' you'd like to strike with God or with another person. "If you do this… I'll do that!" It's as though we're trying to shift responsibility. Taking responsibility will play a major role in coming to terms with loss. This is certainly true in alcohol and drug addiction.

The period of bargaining may include or be followed by a period of depression or low mood. This period of low mood may last for several years.

It is my view that the period of depression is crucial to coming to terms with grief. You may say to me "That is a hard statement." Or you may ask, "Why should that be?"

The period of depression is where one begins to process what has taken place. It is where the fighting, striving and resisting ceases. It is where you gradually come to terms with reality. It is where you begin to see things in a different light. It is where the blame game ends and the bargaining ceases. It is where you begin to accept your loss and to come to terms with it. This was certainly the case for me when overcoming alcohol addiction.

I want to suggest several positive steps you can take to assist in coming to terms the death of someone near: Don't rush; don't fight your feelings; confide in someone you trust; set little targets to aim for; and turn to God.

Don't rush.

When others pressurise you to get on with life, be patient. There isn't a standard, ordained period of time for grieving. You don't have to snap out of it because someone says so. Someday you will no longer want to hold on to your pain. It can be a slow process but you can move beyond your sorrow as Clive and Sylvia did. I'm not saying that you get over it but you can come to a place where you accept your lose.

Don't fight your feelings.

Don't try to bury your feelings, but recognise them, be honest about them and admit them, for something real, painful and important is happening to you. It is acceptable for you to cry and feel sad, whether you are a man or a woman. Don't be taken in by the thought, "I have to be strong for 'so-and-so's' sake". No you don't! You have the right to grieve as much as anyone else does; after all, it is your relative or friend who has died! It may turn out to be of some consolation to 'so-and-so' in the long run that you are grieving too. You might even be able to say, and mean it, "We'll get through this together." Don't try to hide your feelings. Many a person, in later life, has broken down and cried profusely in a counselling room because they never allowed themselves to grieve properly for a particular loved one. This is a tragedy. We should not have to wait a lifetime to grieve. We must never put restrictions on our or another person's right to grieve.

It has also been suggested that putting thoughts into words - writing a letter or poetry can lessen the ache in the heart. No one has to see them you may burn them afterwards if you so wish. It is for you not anyone else that you write things down. Creativity can help you express your feelings, perhaps through playing a musical instrument, painting and drawing or listening to music. Acknowledge your feelings, but do not bury them.

Loneliness is one of the most difficult areas of grieving. You may feel that all you want to do is hide yourself away because no one seems to understand. You feel safe in your room; you can shout and talk to the walls – and no one can ridicule you.

These words strike home the grief one feels at times. So acknowledge your feelings don't bury them.

Confide in someone you trust.

It is important to move beyond the 'four walls' and maybe find someone to talk to, someone in whom you can confide, trust and with whom you may share your grief. Just talking, just listening or maybe just sharing with someone who is simply *there* for you (no strings attached) can be very helpful. Someone who has been there is probably the best person to talk to. Confiding in someone who will rubbish your feelings is not a good person to confide in. So choose wisely, confide in someone you can trust.

Set little targets to aim for.

Setting little targets can be ridiculously simple. To the person who is whole they may seem stupid. Calling on a friend, for instance, can be a massive step for a middle aged or elderly wife who has lost her husband. To have done so is a target you have hit. Cleaning out a cupboard or a wardrobe can be huge because you may find items belonging to your loved one. On the other hand it may be *your own* cupboard and to do so may be therapeutic because you are doing something different and positive. It takes your mind off things for a time. Don't be afraid to do so. You may not want to let go of thoughts of your loved one, but don't be afraid to. you can always return to thoughts of your loved one. Remember, you are not letting your loved one down. Do it one step at a time, little by little. Other things you can do are get tickets for a show or an event you'll enjoy. Start a creative project - painting a picture, writing a poem or a short story. Learn how to knit, make clothes, build plastic models, learn gardening, create your own tropical fish tank or build a model railway. Keeping the mind active will help and doing something for someone else is a means of stepping outside of 'yourself' as I suggested in the chapter Praying for Others.

Turn to God.

After the initial shock and disbelief, above everything else turn to God. Invite Him into your grief. Tell Him how you feel. Do you feel angry? Then tell Him. Are there questions? "God, why did you let this happen?" Are there complaints; "This isn't fair!" Are there doubts; "Are you really there, God?" or "God, where are you?" Then tell Him. Telling God everything is important, even if the questions you ask are 'unanswerable'. He understands our pain and suffers with us; this comes over clearly in Clive and Sylvia's story. Having a faith is helpful in walking through grief. And knowing that we will see our loved one once more can lead to peace and acceptance.

Contemplative prayer can be very helpful when grieving. As we have seen, the whole fabric of contemplative prayer is one of stillness, quiet and of letting go. These are useful attitudes to adopt and useful tools to acquire when grieving. The 'letting go', however, may seem a little scary and there may be a strong feeling of not being quite ready but God doesn't take the whole pain away as though that death never happened. God knows we need to go through the process of grieving. What God can do is make the sorrow, grief and pain a whole load easier to bear. The sorrow, the grief, the sadness, the pain, the 'missing him (or her)' are still there, but nowhere near as crippling as they might have been. Later, with those feelings there will very likely be a sense of joy and pleasure in remembering the good times you shared together. Remember: 'We grieve for what we have lost in order to welcome the future we have in store.'

My take on praying for others, as I have suggested, may also be helpful when grieving, because the shift in focus may kick-start the process, once more, of thinking about someone other than yourself. It is pushing the boat out I know, but worth a go. In one respect it is a simple step to take, but moving outside of yourself and outside of your own immediate circle may appear frightening but it can be so therapeutic. It may have an impact upon your recovery and healing.

Allowing God into your grief any way that you can will help immensely.

To become a stronger person with a deeper appreciation of life than you ever believed possible and to be happy and live life fully again is something that is distant or may seem impossible. To complete that journey would be an amazing outcome. You can achieve it little by little. So don't rush. Don't bury your feelings, but recognise them, be honest about them and admit them, for something real, painful, and important is happening to you.

> *Dear Lord, right now I'm hurting and I can't see any end to it - not in the near future. I look to You now, as I begin to realise that You want to walk with me through this darkness. Metaphorically speaking, I now offer You my hand knowing that Your hand is already outstretched to me. I don't know where I'm going, or what I'm doing, but You know the path that I should take. Lead me in Your path of peace in Jesus' name, and make me a better person with a deeper appreciation of life. Amen. (Prayer written by Rob Giles 2014)*

16

A Question of Depression

"Save me, O God! for the waters have come up to my neck. I sink in deep mire, where there is no standing; I have come into deep waters, where the floods overflow me. I am weary with my crying; my throat is dry; my eyes fail while I wait for my God." (Psalm 69:1-3) "I am troubled, I am bowed down greatly; I go mourning all the day long. For my loins are full of inflammation, and there is no soundness in my flesh. I am feeble and severely broken; I groan because of the turmoil of my heart." (Psalm 38:6-8)

Depression is difficult to define because it is so broad, ranging from being low in spirits in its mildest form through to being life-threatening at its most severe. Individuals suffering from severe clinical depression can often be suicidal. In between these extremes there are also several specific types of depression. Below is a brief overview.

Seasonal Affective Disorder, often called SAD: SAD affects people in the autumn and winter due to lack of sunlight and usually occurs on a regular, annual basis.

Postnatal Depression, which some mothers suffer after giving birth: Many women experience what is known as the 'baby blues' soon after delivery, but it usually passes. Postnatal depression is a more serious condition and can appear any time between two weeks and two years after childbirth.

Bipolar Disorder, previously known as 'manic depression': Individuals with bipolar disorder have mood swings, fluctuating between periods of depression and periods of mania. When manic, and in a state of euphoria, individuals may have grandiose ideas and schemes and may even try to carry them out.

Many people when they're feeling miserable or sad often say, 'I'm feeling depressed' or 'Oh, I am so depressed today'. These feelings, more often than not, are short-lived and soon pass. It is generally accepted by GPs that if the miseries (feelings of sadness and low mood) are persistent and linger for more than two weeks, or if they dominate and interfere with normal everyday living, it may be a sign of depression.

Depression is fairly widespread. Women are much more susceptible to depression than men. This may be due to hormonal imbalance, i.e. monthly cycle or the 'change'. Or it may be due to the fact that men generally find it more difficult to talk about their experiences and admit to being depressed.

Depression is a serious illness and not to be taken lightly. It has been suggested that 1 in 6 people in the UK may experience depression and as many as 1 in 20 may actually be clinically depressed. [26] Individuals suffering from severe clinical depression can often be suicidal, depression being the number one cause of suicide. We dare not take depression lightly. If your body is sick or injured or if you are in pain you would consult a doctor, so why not pay a visit to your GP if your mind is not functioning correctly? The mind is just as much a part of the body as your arms, legs and internal organs... so what is the difference?

It is important to take symptoms seriously and not to dismiss them. There does appear, however, to be some sort of stigma attached to depression and problems associated with mental illness. Many people suffer from depression yet refuse to accept their condition. This is tragic because help is available, but the truth is, no-one can be helped while they're in denial, i.e. in the state of denying the problem. It is important to take symptoms seriously and not to dismiss them.

Symptoms of depression are neither part of growing up nor are they part of growing old as some people think. By recognising the symptoms, getting help and treatment, it is possible to overcome depression.

We may ask, "What symptoms should we look for if we think we may be depressed?" Symptoms of depression are many and varied. For me, the symptoms were as follows:

I was very restless and agitated

I had difficulty staying asleep. I had no problem falling asleep but I was awake all hours of the night.

I felt tired, lacked energy and fell asleep at inappropriate times

I used alcohol more and more

I ate more

I cried excessively

I had physical aches and pains with no physical cause

I was terribly irritable

I felt very low for much of the day and yet at times I experienced moments of euphoria

I placed a lot of guilt upon myself

I blamed myself for my apparent inability to do things

I had interest in sex with my wife but lost the ability to perform

I had difficulty in concentrating and I would procrastinate over the simplest choice

I lacked confidence and self-esteem

I was overcome by negative thoughts

I felt empty, helpless and full of despair

I felt that my situation was hopeless

I could not see any future for me

I had thoughts of suicide

For a more comprehensive list of symptoms visit the Mind website. [27]

People who are depressed are often very anxious and may suffer from panic attacks. Our minds very likely will become full of thoughts and questions that cannot be resolved. Some suffer from headaches and migraines, aching muscles, dizzy spells and vertigo as was my experience. Physically speaking, one can feel drained and generally unwell.

You might ask, "What causes depression?" There is no one thing which causes depression. It varies from one individual to another. It may be a combination of factors. For instance it could be traumatic experiences such as the death of a loved one, an accident or illness, being fired or made redundant. All of these can cause depression.

Depression could also be the result of an underactive thyroid, so if depression cannot be accounted for by life changes, then it is important to consult your medical practitioner. Other things that can cause depression are poor diet, lack of physical fitness or influenza.

People with depression show changes to chemical messengers in the brain known as neurotransmitters. These are the parts of the body that are not functioning correctly when we are depressed. What is not clear is whether these cause depression or whether they are the product of depression. What is clear, however, is that depression can feed itself. When we are depressed we can be depressed about being depressed and so it becomes a vicious circle. Depression in these circumstances can be more problematic than the difficulties that caused it in the first place. To break the cycle is not easy, for negative thoughts are automatic and, as such, they're difficult to challenge. Nevertheless, one has to break the hold that depression has by challenging negative thoughts and negative feelings. Cognitive behaviour therapy (CBT) may be helpful for those who are not severely depressed.

Again, contemplative prayer may also be very helpful as I discovered myself, first hand. The whole fabric of contemplative prayer is one of calm, quiet and peace, of letting go, releasing to God and changing thought patterns. These are the right conditions, attitudes and tools necessary to challenge negative thoughts.

Praying for others in the way I have suggested in a previous chapter can be extremely helpful too. When a person is depressed they are generally absorbed in their own personal crisis or world of woe. When a person is depressed it isn't easy to pray for someone, in the ordinary sense of praying. One easily gets distracted, disillusioned and overcome by the magnitude of one's own burden. However, by using our own crisis, burden and misery, inserting others into our prayers can be very uplifting. The deliberate shift of focus from our own misery to thinking and praying for someone else can be very effective in challenging negative thoughts.

The National Institute for Clinical Excellence (NICE) suggests that medication is the appropriate way forward for those who are severely depressed. [28] Antidepressants are available and designed to stimulate the neurotransmitters in the brain that aren't working properly. Because these neurotransmitters are not functioning correctly, the brains of those who are severely depressed pick up wrong signals and wrong messages. Antidepressants are given to address that problem and not, as some think, to dope up the individual so they become like a zombie. Help is available. Ask for it, accept it. You do not have to suffer. And, above all else, pray. Open your heart and allow God into your healing programme.

> *Dear Lord, while I'm finding it difficult to think and to understand what's going on, be with me, help me and care for me. Show me the things that I, myself, can do to effect change in my life. Teach me how I may change my thinking. Help me, Holy Spirit, to train my mind and keep it fixed upon Jesus, so that 'I may abide in You and You may abide in me'. Lift me up out of these doldrums in Jesus' name. Amen. (Prayer written by Rob Giles 2014)*

17

A Question of Pain

"Turn Yourself to me, and have mercy on me, for I am desolate and afflicted. The troubles of my heart have enlarged; bring me out of my distresses! Look on my affliction and my pain, and forgive all my sins." (Psalm 25:16-18)

The Bible has very little to say about pain. There are references to the pains of childbirth, the pains of sin, and the pains of punishment, but precious little else. There aren't any direct Scriptures to say that God will heal our pain. Nevertheless, when the damaged part of our body is healed, our pain generally disappears. Pain is very much a part of life, although we might not want to view it as such. You may say to me, "Whoa! That's a strong statement!" So let us take a closer look.

Pain isn't pleasant and I'm not suggesting for one moment that it is. The Collins Dictionary and Thesaurus defines pain as: *"The sensation of acute physical hurt or discomfort caused by injury or illness."* [29]

All of us will experience some form of pain in our lifetime, whether it is mental, physical or emotional. If pain did not exist we would not be alerted to a problem. We would put ourselves in great danger of seriously damaging ourselves. Pain motivates us to recoil from potentially damaging situations. For instance, where there is fire we will move with caution so as not to burn ourselves. And again when using power tools we will handle them with care so as not to cut or damage vulnerable parts of our body. Pain will also prompt us to withdraw in order to protect a wound or an injury, while we allow it to heal. Pain, too, is useful to the physician in the diagnosis of a potential problem.

Most pain is resolved when the painful stimulus is removed or the part of the body in question has healed. I am, of course, stating the obvious, but sometimes pain will persist even when the body has healed. Pain may also arise in the absence of any detectable stimulus, damage or disease. Pain is a major symptom in many medical conditions and can interfere significantly with a person's general quality of life and their ability to function properly. It is no fun at all when you are in constant pain, hour after hour, day after day but pain, nevertheless, is a gift from God.

There is acute pain and there is chronic pain. Acute pain is usually short term. Examples are: child-birth, fracturing a bone, stubbing a toe, hitting a thumb with a hammer, cutting a finger with a knife, etc. etc. These things are extremely painful initially, but very soon the pain decreases and will disappear altogether when that particular part of the body has healed. For instance, a toe is incredibly painful immediately it is stubbed, but even after a short period of time the pain will begin to subside to a point where it becomes bearable; in two or three days the toe is usually back to normal.

Chronic pain is long term. Examples are: advanced cancer pain, rheumatoid arthritis, gall-stones, arthritis, rheumatism, fibromyalgia etc. etc.

Pain relief medication may be given for both acute and chronic pain conditions. It is given so that the pain becomes manageable, but rarely will it result in removing the pain completely. There are many types of pain relief medication; it is important to consult your GP or health care professional in order to find what is right and appropriate for you. In addition, there are many alternative medications and alternative therapies available which can be very helpful too, but again, it is always wise to consult your GP first.

When pain is in the foreground, it dominates our thinking and dominates our lives, and greatly reduces our functionality. A technique used in Cognitive Behaviour Therapy (CBT) and also in the Expert Patients Programme (EPP), is 'distraction'. Distraction techniques are activities that distract the mind, taking it away from the pain. Examples of these could be artistic, such as painting, drawing, or writing or pursuits such as gardening, fishing, bird-watching, playing a musical instrument or indeed any activity that we enjoy. The therapy of painting, for instance, has been used to great effect among veterans of war suffering from post-traumatic stress disorder.

There have been many who have found playing a musical instrument to be a great distraction to pain. Many who have felt positively ill and in pain have played their instrument along with a group of other musicians and felt invigorated as they have in some way lost themselves in the music. An example of this is Keith Richards of the Rolling Stones. His fingers, if you notice, are badly arthritic and they must be very painful under normal circumstances yet he can stand and play a two hour concert and get lost in the music. Endorphins, the body's natural opiates, so we are told, are released during such activities, thus giving us the 'feel-good factor'. They bring with them relief from pain, albeit for a brief period.

Praying for others in the way that I have prescribed can also be beneficial. Taking your own pain or discomfort and using it as a *suggestion* to lead you into a time of prayer can be a great help. Praying for and thinking of someone in pain, other than yourself, is a great distraction when dealing with pain. The Holy Spirit too, can use it and we ourselves may get lost in a time of intercession.

I've used the word *suggestion* because that is all it is meant to be, nothing more. Allow your pain to *suggest* to you people or situations into which you may pray. Be clear on this. You aren't experiencing the *same* pain as those for whom you are praying; this exercise merely gives you a point of *association*. View it in these terms and you will not go wrong. But should you begin thinking that you are feeling or experiencing the same as those for whom you are praying, you will be off-beam and will have missed the point. It is not a magic formula, merely a *suggestion*, a point of *association*, leading to a welcome distraction and possible blessing for others.

The practice of contemplative prayer may also be helpful. The quiet, the stillness and the oneness of the heart with God, can be so very beautiful that it can lift the mind and the spirit above the pain. The pain may still be there but in terms of our *thinking*, it is in the background rather than the foreground. This, I think, is a more subtle form of distraction. The reality of God that contemplation brings is more than just a tonic or a lifeline; it is actually life itself.

Recently I came across the eulogy that Joseph de Beaufort, Vicar General to the Archbishop of Paris, delivered at the funeral of Brother Lawrence in the late 17th Century. Some readers will no doubt be familiar with Brother Lawrence through having read his little book entitled, "Practicing the Presence of God". De Beaufort's eulogy is actually found as the foreword to one of the several translations of that book. [30]

Brother Lawrence, as we discover, practised contemplative prayer and his whole life became one of devotion and talking constantly with God. Joseph de Beaufort, in his eulogy, said that Lawrence had suffered for around twenty five years with a form of sciatic gout as well as an ulcerated leg causing him 'acute pain'. This, of course, took place in an age before modern medicine. De Beaufort goes on to talk of three major illnesses that Lawrence suffered before his death in 1691.

Of Lawrence's responses to the third illness, de Beaufort wrote:

"He showed the marks of extraordinary constancy, resignation, and joy." [31]

If de Beaufort has chosen the last four words carefully, then we may assume according to definition, that Lawrence, in his *constancy*, was unchanging, resolute and steadfast. In his *resignation* he displayed a submissive unresisting attitude and in his *joy*, was happy and content, displaying pleasure and delight and true satisfaction. You may want to exclaim, "The man was surely out of his mind!!" But I would answer, "No, he wasn't out of his mind". He'd simply found God to be his 'all-in-all'. He'd found God to be sufficient even in the midst of extreme suffering. De Beaufort wrote:

"He never seemed to have a moment of distress in the greatest violence of his illness. His joy appeared not only on his face, but in his manner of speaking as well." [32]

This is quite extraordinary, for pain generally affects both our countenance and our speech. Pain is very difficult to disguise, but I'm not so sure that we really want to disguise it either. We like to feel a little sympathy or to feel that someone cares when we are in pain. Lawrence, however, found a 'place' or 'position' in God, where, in calm and quiet, his spirit could rise above the agonies of his suffering.

Contemplative prayer is a great tool not only for drawing near to God but also as a simple, yet effective, means of managing discomfort and pain. I'm not saying that discomfort or pain will go away, but I am saying that touching God in silent prayer may enable us to bear it.

You might ask, "Why is that?"

We are, of course, yielding our pain and discomfort to Him when we pray in contemplation. More than that - we are seeking an inner stillness, whereby we are undisturbed by discomfort, cares and anxieties; we are looking beyond our pain and our suffering, in order to know God more intimately.

Contemplative prayer will bring about changes that will astonish anyone who is of the mind to use its simplicity. The reality of God that it brings will delight anyone's heart. Thankfulness is a great acquisition. It may sound odd but developing thankfulness and gratitude in the midst of our difficulties and pain can be a wonderful gift from God. Thanksgiving can break a grumbling and complaining heart and lift our spirits to an amazing height, as we will see from the following three chapters. That is, if we have the courage to use it for our advantage.

> *Dear Lord, I have heard strange (paradoxical) things and yet I sense their truth and reality. To find You, moment by moment each day, would be so reassuring. I ask You, therefore, dear Lord to lead me. I can only look to You and ask… "Lord, help me. Take my life and lead me deeper into You through prayer. Will You bring the light of revelation to my eyes and the peace that will garrison my heart?" In Jesus' name Amen. (Prayer written by Rob Giles 2014)*

18

Praying with Thanksgiving (1)

"Oh, give thanks to the Lord! Call upon His name; make known His deeds among the peoples! Sing to him, sing psalms to Him; talk of all his wondrous works!" (Psalm 105:1&2) "Praise the Lord! Oh, give thanks to the Lord, for He is good! For His mercy endures forever." (Psalm 106:1)

The Apostle Paul in his first letter to Timothy seemingly placed prayer into categories when he wrote: *"...I exhort first of all that supplications, prayers, intercessions, and giving of thanks be made for all men,"* (1Timothy 2:1). In this passage he identified four specific types of prayer that we may use when praying for others. Each has its own place and particular part to play in our experience and each is tailored for different situations and circumstances. Most of us are familiar with *supplications, prayers and intercessions*. We're familiar too with the *'giving of thanks'*, although we may not have identified it as a category of prayer in its own right.

At the beginning of nearly all his epistles, Paul gives thanks for those to whom his letters were addressed: *"First, I thank my God through Jesus Christ for you all..." (Romans 1:8) "I thank my God always concerning you..." (1 Corinthians 1:4) "I... do not cease to give thanks for you, making mention of you in my prayers: (Ephesians 1:16). "I thank my God upon every remembrance of you," (Philippians 1:3). "We give thanks to the God and Father of our Lord Jesus Christ, praying always for you," (Colossians 1:3). "We give thanks to God always for you all, making mention of you in our prayers," (1 Thessalonians 1:2). "We are bound to thank God always for you..." (2 Thessalonians 1:3). "I thank my God, making mention of you always in my prayers," (Philemon 4)...* His letters are also strewn elsewhere with spontaneous outbursts of thanksgiving, rejoicing, gratitude and praise. Paul laid a great deal of emphasis upon the *art* of being thankful.

Now I say 'art', because art is by definition:

"The quality, production, expression, or realm, according to aesthetic principles, of what is beautiful, appealing, or of more than ordinary significance" [33]

Thankfulness is an *extra* ordinary expression that meets all the above criteria for there is none so beautiful and appealing as a person who is thankful; such people are a pleasure to be with. Thankfulness is a pure emotion that defies intellectuality. In my view, thankfulness is an aesthetic quality of high significance but sadly lacking in the lives of many of God's people today. That is an observation and not a criticism.

One of the keys to both a healthy mindset and a healthy attitude is thankfulness. Some Christians are naturally thankful and positively cheery; some are negative, critical and cynical, to whom thankfulness and gratitude do not come easily. And yet, all of us may develop thankfulness. As Paul said elsewhere, *"Let the peace of Christ keep you in tune with each other, in step with each other. None of this going off and doing your own thing. And cultivate thankfulness." (Colossians 3:15 The Message).* Paul said *'cultivate thankfulness'*. He would never have said those words if it wasn't possible. You might say to me, "How then can we cultivate thankfulness and gratitude?" The answer is quite straightforward - simply begin to include some form of thanksgiving in your prayers! This may seem a little patronising and overly simplistic - but it works! For those who are locked into a negative mindset, there is no other way out.

On a personal note: I had been a Christian for approximately thirty years when, as I have described elsewhere, around the turn of the millennium I had a mental and emotional breakdown. As you are aware, in my quest to cope, I turned more and more to alcohol. My drink problem, which had formerly been manageable (up to a point), slowly turned into one that was unmanageable - I became addicted to alcohol. I had also been depressed for several years prior to that breakdown but I hadn't associated depression with my condition. I would have said a thousand times - "I'm not depressed". But the depression worsened. The result, mentally and emotionally, was devastating and I feared insanity. As one might expect, my personality darkened. I became angry, despondent, miserable and grumpy, partly due to the frustration of not having the mental and emotional resources to cope and partly because I was also just plain angry. In my depression, thankfulness to God for what I had, who I was and for people in my life, was virtually non-existent. Why am I saying this?

In the autumn of 2004 I had an encounter with God that changed my life; many things changed overnight. However, some things did not. One of the things that did not change, would you believe, was my grumpy and thankless attitude. In due course, however, by some miracle, by the mercies of God, I discovered a means of cultivating thankfulness. I simply made a deliberate choice to say 'thank you' to God in my prayers.

I began by ascribing to God everyday things that took place in my life. Things I would, ordinarily, have overlooked such as finding a parking place at a busy time of day, finding things I had misplaced, being aware of different flavours while eating, different smells when entering a room (or the fragrance of a lady passing by in the street!), orders coming in for work just when I needed them and for the providence that appeared so real the more I gave thanks. I'm not sure if I was developing thanksgiving *per se*, or whether I was developing 'mindfulness' of being thankful. Either way, thankfulness gradually became part of my life and brought with it a certain amount of healing to my thankless heart. This 'healing' was a *bonus*, as I hadn't set out with that particular goal in mind.

Whenever we give thanks with God in mind, whether it is for what we have or for what we receive, or whether it's simply giving thanks for people who play a major role in our lives, we are giving recognition and appreciation to God. The more we give thanks with the voice, the greater the likelihood of gratitude growing in our hearts.

For those like me who are of a negative disposition,

by actually giving thanks, we are encouraging gratitude, as an entity, to blossom and bear fruit in our lives. *"...Do you not know that a little leaven leavens the whole lump?" (1 Corinthians 5:6)* [Leaven refers to a lump of sourdough retained from previous bread-making, a practice they still employ on the Continent instead of yeast.] That Scriptural analogy certainly applies to thanksgiving. Just a little thanksgiving will, in time, dispel negative, cynical and grumpy attitudes, if we are of a mind to use it, work at it and work with it.

It isn't difficult to become miserable, but it is difficult to break free once we are. My advice is, start small. Say 'thank you' to God for something – anything. Once you have begun, don't give up. Say 'thank you' for something else, then thank Him for something else - something else, and something else... Over time, as you persist, remarkable changes *will* take place.

At first you may have to fight to give thanks, go out of your way to give thanks, and deny yourself any invitation to a 'pity party' in order to give thanks. (My plea is never indulge in self-pity because it can be so damaging.) There is no easy way round this. You may even have to force yourself to become mindful of God in everyday things, as I did. But after a while you will find that it will come naturally - you will automatically be more mindful of the blessings of God... you will automatically become more thankful for what you have... more thankful for who you are.... and more thankful for just being alive. This may appear to be overly simplistic as I have already said but, believe me, it does work. It is a powerful and life-changing exercise.

Some people will say that you are living a lie and

denying reality by forcing yourself to give thanks when you do not feel like it. "You are putting on a front!" They might say, "You are wearing a mask!" because they perceive you are not giving thanks to God with a pure heart. "It's like being thankful by way of being polite, courteous and exercising good manners; and yet not being genuinely thankful from the heart."

I say no! No, you're not! How else will you ever break free from thanklessness unless you first begin to actually give thanks?! Is gratitude to God going to come down from heaven, slap you in the face, wake you up, and suddenly change your life? I think not! When we give thanks to God, whether it is heartfelt or forced, we are taking a giant stride to meet God; and all of us may be certain of this one thing… God will take two strides to our one to meet us.

On a personal note: I had worked in industry for thirty four years prior to my breakdown. Just after the turn of the millennium but during my journey to recovery from alcoholism, I started my own small business. I was self-employed and traded as a carpenter. My job took me into the homes of people and I enjoyed that aspect of my work very much.

One morning, travelling to a customer, I had to take a right turn into a country lane which took me through a dark avenue of trees. It was a beautiful sunny morning and as my little van emerged from what seemed like a dark tunnel into the bright sunshine, I was struck by what I can only describe as a moment of *God-consciousness*. That moment turned into an explosion of thankfulness, wonder and praise. My window was down. I was aware.... *extra* ordinarily aware, of the smell of fresh air, green grass and flowers. I could see the beauty of the countryside and hear the birds singing. All of my senses were touched; I felt so alive and seized by the contrast between this precious moment and that of my former life in industry. I felt that God had been so very good to me over the previous nine months as I had striven with Him to overcome my depression and render thanks to Him whether I felt like it or not.

Formerly, when I worked in industry, I rarely saw the light of day. For almost five months of the year I travelled to work and back in the dark. During that period of time I felt imprisoned by long hours in what seemed to be a mundane, 'soul-destroying' job. Now, however, working for myself, I was free - that reality suddenly dawned. It 'broke in' upon me in similar fashion to my van 'breaking out' of the dark tunnel of trees into the bright sunshine. It was a moment when heaven seemed so very close. Gratitude flooded my being and I was punching the air and shouting, "Yes! Yes! Yes! Praise God! Praise God! Praise God!"

During the nine months prior to this event, as I have intimated, I had been giving thanks and often *fighting* to give thanks, even though I didn't feel like it. I had been trying to wade through the swamp of my depression and fight for a sound mind by giving thanks to God. I gave thanks even though it wasn't real and it didn't appear to be true in my experience. I had in fact been *praying with thanksgiving* although I hadn't realised it. I had taken but one difficult step to meet God.... but now God had taken several steps to meet me, and quite out of the blue, burst in upon me. At that point, I was bearing the fruit of all the thanksgiving I had sown over the previous nine months. The reality of it all had finally caught up with me.

Thanksgiving had been therapy to me and had brought with it the healing I so desperately needed. Even now, ten years on, I occasionally have to fight to give thanks, but I am determined to do so; I do not want to end up miserable, grumpy and as thankless as I once was or worse.

Do we have the courage to take *one small step* of faith - and thank God regardless? I sincerely hope so.

Heavenly Father, enable me to spot the small things that take place in my life, so that I may begin to render thanks to You. Help me to discern the things that You have provided and I have taken for granted. I'm sorry that I have failed to spot many things which are clearly from Your hand of kindness. I give You thanks now for all that You have done, all that You are doing and all that You are going to do, in the wonderful name of Jesus, Amen. (Prayer written by Rob Giles 2014)

19

Praying with Thanksgiving (2)

"In everything give thanks; for this is the will of God in Christ Jesus for you." (1Thessalonians 5:18) "Giving thanks always for all things to God the Father in the name of our Lord Jesus Christ," (Ephesians 5:20).

Those four words, *'in everything give thanks'*, mean we should give thanks in whatever situation or in whatsoever circumstance we find ourselves. I am of course stating the obvious for there is no ambiguity in the Apostle's exhortation. Some might say in the light of that, "Isn't Paul going a little too far?" Others might object saying, "You don't know what I'm going through!" "I've just lost my job...." "My wife's just left me...." "My husband has just been diagnosed...." "This sort of Christian ideal is OK in theory but it cannot work in practice!" or "It's alright for people like Mother Teresa but surely it's out of reach for the average Christian!?" Sadly, to most of us it does appear to be out of reach and even unacceptable. But, if what we are saying is true, then thankfulness should be achievable by everyone.

When the problems we face are transformed into insurmountable or immoveable difficulties, thankfulness is crowded out and stifled. Often when we're engulfed in life's problems and we are fearful and anxious, our human understanding, thinking and judgements become clouded and we sink into the doldrums. At such moments, we must learn to *fight* back by finding something to thank God for, or else run the risk of being overwhelmed. I sometimes have to stop and think to myself; "No! I'm not going to allow myself to be swamped by this problem!" "I do not feel like thanking God, but I am going to thank Him anyway!"

There is an element of risk in giving thanks.

The risk lies in the fact that there are no guarantees our situation will change. It becomes a risk because of the uncertainties... "What happens next?" or "Where does this leave us now?" or "Where do we go from here?" We may be certain of this, however: thankfulness *will* change our attitude even though our problems may remain the same.

Giving thanks in every situation is a discipline.

It is a discipline because it involves training. If thanksgiving doesn't come naturally, then you will have to work at it. It's like breaking old habits and forming new ones or like an athlete training for a competition. When it hurts, when it doesn't come easily or when you don't feel like doing it, you still have to press through and do it anyway.

Giving thanks in every situation is an offering.

It is an offering you and I may give to God anytime

Where Heaven Touches Earth

we choose. When we don't feel like giving thanks but we do it anyway, it becomes a *sacrifice of thanksgiving*. The psalmist said: *"I will offer to you the sacrifice of thanksgiving, and will call upon the name of the Lord." (Psalm 116:17)* It is not a sacrifice unless it costs. When Araunah the Jebusite offered to give his own threshing floor and oxen to David in order that sacrifice might be made to God, David replied, *"…No, but I will surely buy it from you for a price; nor will I offer burnt offerings to the Lord my God with that which costs me nothing…" (2 Samuel 24:24)* David understood the principle that the most meaningful sacrifices are the ones that cost. I think of the 'widow's two mites' *(see Mark 12:42-44)*. This widow dropped two insignificant and seemingly worthless coins into the Temple Treasury but Jesus recognised their great worth inasmuch as she had given *all* her living.

Giving thanks in every situation is the will of God.

The Scripture says; *"In everything give thanks; for this is the will of God in Christ Jesus for you." (1Thessalonians 5:17)* I'm sure that every believer has the desire to perform the will of God. Thanksgiving then, is but one simple way of complying with God's will. It's not as though Paul is asking us to go to the ends of the earth or to do something outrageous and unreasonable! All he asks is that we render thanks to God *in everything*! Doing the will of God is like any other Christian virtue; once you begin it will, over the course of time, become an integral part of who you are.

The Apostle Paul, in his letter to the Ephesians said, *"Giving thanks always for all things to God the Father in the name of our Lord Jesus Christ," (Ephesians 5:20)*. Now notice, please, the difference between "**in** *everything* *give thanks"* and *"giving thanks always **for** all things."* It is between those two words *in* and *for*. When Paul said *"**in** everything give thanks"*, he meant giving thanks in every situation and in every circumstance. When he said *"giving thanks always **for** all things"*, he meant giving thanks for the good and for the bad. Job said, *"...Shall we indeed accept good from God, and shall we not accept adversity?..." (Job 2:10).*

Someone might say, "Surely, Job is out of his mind!" But actually no, no he's not. If you think about it seriously his reasoning is quite sound. What Job is saying, in effect, is this: "When life throws up good things, I *will* receive them as receiving them from the hand of my God; when life throws up hardships and tribulation, I *will* accept them as they are, place my hand in the hand of the Saviour and we will walk through them together".

To give thanks to God *for all things* may seem ridiculous to the intellect and might, on the face of it, appear to be bad teaching. But if we have the courage to do it, we would very soon discover something quite extraordinary taking place - our persistent thanksgiving unveiling a sense of contentment in our lives. That is a big, big claim. But think about it for one moment; there is no way that anyone could be thankful *for the good* and *for the bad* unless they were content.

Mistakenly we think, "If my circumstances changed, then I would be content!" "If this happened... or if that happened!" "If I had this... or if I had that, then I'd be happy and content!" But it doesn't work that way! Paul said, *"...I have learned in whatever state I am, to be content: I know how to be abased, and I know how to abound. Everywhere and in all things I have learned both to be full and to be hungry, both to abound and suffer need." (Philippians 4:11&12)* How did he *learn* that kind of contentment? He learnt it by simply giving thanks and showing gratitude to God in *the good times* and in *the bad times*. It is our heart and our thinking that must change, not our circumstances. Contentment is the product of submission to God in life's difficulties and it is the fruit of thankfulness, praise and gratitude to God.

On a personal note: I have a friend who gives audible praise to God whenever things go wrong. The first words upon her lips invariably are, "Praise the Lord". I recall one time she had forgotten that her cakes were in the oven. When she finally opened the oven door, the cakes were burnt. She exclaimed out loud, 'Praise the Lord'! You might be thinking, "What on earth's going on here?!" But by giving audible praise to God, she was placing the situation totally into His hands... and God is greater than any situation. It was with joy and sheer delight in God that she was able to rescue one or two of her burnt cakes. (I was fortunate to sample one of the 'rescued' cakes)

By giving audible praise to God, she was closing the door on the devil. She had in effect pulled the rug from under his feet. Shrewd move... for the Scripture says, *"...do not let the sun go down on your wrath, nor give place to the devil." (Ephesians 4:26&27)*. By giving audible praise to God, she was also stopping herself from swearing or getting angry. When she placed the burnt cakes in the bin, in her mind that incident was over and there was no room for a *pity party...* she was moving on without resentment. In no time at all she was calm and thanking God with genuine praise.

This may seem laughable of course, but I witnessed her panic melt into gratitude in a matter of moments. I witnessed a potentially explosive situation transformed by self-control. We do not hear much about self-control these days; it's not a particularly *'cool'* topic. Sadly when we throw a tantrum, curse and swear, all we are doing is giving the devil a foothold. She exercised self-control by offering audible praise to God at a time when normal responses would possibly have caused her to lose her *cool* and cast aside her *dignity*. The way she dealt with this situation was to prove to be very decisive and a very valuable lesson indeed.

One morning her youngest son went into his sister's room for some item or other and casually dropped his cigarette-butt into the waste bin as he left the room. Unknown to anyone, there was an empty aerosol can of hair-spray in the bin. The bin eventually caught fire and the can exploded like a grenade. My friend bounded up the stairs. Seeing the flames leaping up the wall and the curtains on fire, she ran along the landing screaming, *"Praise the Lord! Praise the Lord! Praise the Lord!"* She ran into the toilet, grabbed a towel, soaked it with cold water, threw it over the flaming waste bin and snuffed out the fire. In the event, the extent of the damage was fairly minimal - burnt curtains, a damaged window frame, a badly singed carpet and smoke-damaged wallpaper and ceiling… a far cry from what might have been!

Later when relating the story, she was full of praise and adoration to God. Her story was all about what God had done… and not about what she had done. How He had saved the day… how He had saved them from disaster... how He had given her the wisdom to know what to do.

The idea that it is bad teaching to give thanks to God *in everything* and to give thanks *always for all things* is, frankly, quite ludicrous when we have at our disposal a simple and yet profound means of *overcoming*. I'm not suggesting that we do exactly as my friend did but I am suggesting allowing thankfulness, gratitude and praise to become a part of our everyday lives.

The principle of thankfulness is a major step forward to effect personal change. Why should we be defined by bad responses? Why should we have to swear? Why should we have to use expletives? Why should we allow the devil to walk all over us? Why shouldn't we be content? Why shouldn't we exercise self-control? Why shouldn't we *choose* to be thankful? How else may we break free from the miseries?! How else may we turn away from anger and the sense of injustice we feel when things go wrong?!

Heavenly Father, now I'm beginning to see that some of the Christian virtues like contentment and self-control may be achieved through thankfulness. Mistakenly, I have thought that I could only ever aspire to contentment but never actually achieve it. Forgive me, I was wrong. Help me now to go deeper in showing my gratitude and thankfulness to You in the situations I find myself. I'm looking forward to seeing changes taking place in my life through your amazing grace. Amen. (Prayer written by Rob Giles 2014)

20

Praying with Thanksgiving (3)

"I will bless the Lord at all times; His praise shall continually be in my mouth. My soul shall make its boast in the Lord; the humble shall hear of it and be glad. Oh magnify the Lord with me, and let us exalt His name together. I sought the Lord, and he heard me, and delivered me from all my fears." (Psalm 34:1-4)

In the book of Proverbs it says, *"A merry heart makes a cheerful countenance..." (Proverbs 15:13)* A cheerful countenance comes from within; it comes from the heart. A merry heart and a cheerful countenance will not only perk us up individually but will affect those around us.

It also says in the book of Proverbs, *"A merry heart does good, like a medicine..." (Proverbs 17:22)* When we're in the presence of those who are cheerful, we are more likely to become cheerful ourselves. If we spend an evening in side-splitting laughter at a show, we'll more than likely return home in a good frame of mind.

Laughter is like a medicine and it works wonders but, in contrast, *"...a broken spirit dries the bones." (Proverbs 17:22)* It is true to say that we don't always *feel* like rejoicing but we can, however, *choose* to be cheerful. A merry heart is a powerful agent to effect personal change.

Again on a personal note: my friend Wilf is inspirational... he's always cheerful. He's now in his ninetieth year and has recently been registered blind but this is not a hindrance to him, nor does it deter him. In his company laughter is part of the course... it's contagious. He's the type of fellow who doesn't take himself too seriously and always sees the funny side of his own misfortunes.

His sister Ruth, who sadly has since passed away, lived in a care home some 180 miles from his home in the Midlands (UK). When she was taken seriously ill and not expected to live many days, he made the trip to visit her. He travelled alone by train, without assistance from the rail network. With no direct train from Stourbridge to Portsmouth he would have to change trains at least twice - at Worcester and again at Bath Spa. This was his chosen option as the other options involved at least three changes. Upon arrival at Worcester he was informed that the train to Bath Spa had been cancelled; all passengers would therefore have to catch a bus to Cheltenham Spa and from there take the train to Portsmouth, changing once more en route at Bristol. This would have been stressful for any 88 year-old, yet he took it all in his stride and regarded it as an *adventure*.

Upon arrival at Portsmouth, other passengers being courteous ushered him to the doorway of the train. Due to his blindness, he couldn't find the button to open the door and the train pulled away leaving him and half-a-dozen passengers to get off at the next stop and make their own way back to Portsmouth. That evening he telephoned to let me know he'd arrived safely. His first words were, "Life is getting a little too exciting for an old chap!" and with that he burst into raucous laughter before relating his *adventure* to me.

Wilf wasn't always this way. I can remember him suffering at least three major bouts of depression. One of which was so serious my wife and I thought we might lose him. With the right medication, however, he has bounced back, choosing to be cheerful and to laugh at life. There is much to be said for laughter.

Isaiah said, *"...to give them beauty for ashes, the oil of joy for mourning, the garments of praise for the spirit of heaviness; that they may be called the trees of righteousness, the planting of the Lord, that He may be glorified." (Isaiah 61:3)*

You might ask, "Why use the metaphor of a garment of praise?" Often the situations we find ourselves in are such that we do not feel like praising God or being cheerful. At times like these, God encourages us... "Come on! Stir yourself up and put on a cheery countenance, just as you would a nice clean garment." God likens praise to a garment, but like any other garment, it does no good hidden away in a closet or wardrobe; we must put it on to feel its benefit and display its beauty.

The Apostle Paul said, *"Rejoice in the Lord always. Again I will say rejoice!" (Philippians 4:4)* In another place he said, *"Rejoice always, pray without ceasing," (1 Thessalonians 5:16&17).* I believe these verses are exhortations, demonstrating that we have both the right and the power to *choose*. To do so, however, we may have to turn our back on the injustices we feel regarding our current situation. Other times we must disregard our resentment by releasing it to God. Nevertheless, we do have the power to choose. We can say... "This is an awful situation but I'm not going to let it grind me down; I will *choose* to be cheerful and I *will* give God the glory."

We can be certain of one thing; a cheerful, praiseworthy response does bring glory to God. Isaiah said in the passage we have just read, *"... that they may be called the trees of righteousness, the planting of the Lord, that He may be glorified." (Isaiah 61:3)*

Again on a personal note: I am the type of person who is not normally of a cheerful disposition. I have an illness called fibromyalgia; it's a strange condition with varied symptoms that are a nuisance more than anything else. It isn't life-threatening, but it does knock me about from time to time. For instance, I'm now unable to sleep at night without a sedative and most of the time I'm uncomfortable with irritable bowel and irritable bladder syndromes. Some days I feel positively ill. Other days I ache all over and my body is tender to the touch or else I'm restricted in movement by the tightening of the muscles and aggravated by painful tendonitis or sciatica. On occasions I'm exhausted, exhibiting 'flu-like symptoms. And there are times when my brain is *foggy* and I'm dysfunctional in memory, co-ordination and cognition. But I have made the choice to be cheerful. I have to put *cheerfulness* on. To be quite honest, sometimes it is literally - a *'put on'*, where cheerfulness does not appear real at all to me.

You might say to me, "You're living a lie!" "You aren't being true to yourself!" But I think to myself, "Who cares? I'm going to attempt to be cheerful anyway!" I am learning from experience that the only way to be cheerful is to *start* being cheerful.

The Apostle Paul said: *"Rejoice in Lord always. Again I will say rejoice." (Philippians 4:4)*

Recently I read a magazine article telling the harrowing story of Alan Benson, a pastor and missionary working near the border of China and Inner Mongolia during the Second World War. [34]

His story is quite disturbing. He was arrested on the 27th of August 1940 by occupying Japanese forces, on charges of spying. Twelve hours a day for seven weeks he was beaten and tortured by his captors as they tried to extract a confession. Then his captors turned to the water torture by holding him down, gagging him and pouring salt water into his nostrils. When his captors realised he could not sleep they turned to brain washing him. Alan prayed that God would take away the pain and give him the grace to be able to face the demands of the following day. When he rose to his feet he found the agonising pain had left his body. He was so thrilled he began to dance around his cell praising God. The moment that Alan began to dance around his cell was a moment when *heaven touched earth*.

In the most adverse of circumstances, God broke into the life of Alan Benson causing him to rejoice. As Peter puts it, *"... Though now you do not see Him, yet believing, you rejoice with joy inexpressible and full of glory." (1Peter 1:8)*

You or I are unlikely to endure anything of the magnitude or the horror that Alan suffered. Generally speaking, we in the West possess freedoms that allow us to bask in the blessings of God... we have so much to be thankful for and yet we still grumble and complain from time to time.

So I say; surely we can find something for which to render thanks to God! Surely we can muster the courage from somewhere to give God the glory! If we don't do this, we may never break the cycle of misplaced reasoning, negativity, doubt, confusion and failure. Thankfulness, praise and rejoicing are powerful weapons in the Christian's armoury; we should not underestimate their power and we should not shun their use.

Father God, grant me the courage that will enable me to give You the thanks and praise. Here I am! I'm still standing and I'm still alive! Help me to change my thinking and bring glory to Your name. Amen. (Prayer written by Rob Giles 2014)

21

A Question of Abuse

"...And Tamar took the cakes which she had made, and brought them to Amnon her brother in the bedroom. Now when she had brought them to him to eat, he took hold of her and said to her, 'Come, lie with me, my sister.' But she answered him, 'No, my brother, do not force me, for no such thing should be done in Israel. Do not do this disgraceful thing! And I, where could I take my shame? And as for you, you would be like one of the fools in Israel...' However, he would not heed her voice; and being stronger than she, he forced her and he lay with her." (2 Samuel 13:10-14) *"...the men would not heed him. So the man took his concubine and brought her out to them. And they knew her and abused her all night until morning; and when the day began to break, they let her go."* (Judges 19:25)

Abuse comes in many forms. It may be designated by these terms: physical, sexual, verbal, psychological and spiritual.

Physical abuse includes practices such as bullying,

Where Heaven Touches Earth

domestic violence, maltreatment, beating, burning and neglect, to name but a few. It is difficult to imagine such practices going on within a family unit, yet the tragedy is sometimes they do.

All forms of sexual abuse are vile practices. They are sins against God and they are crimes against humanity. In fact, all forms of sexual activity outside the confines of marriage are wrong and they are sins against God. Now, you may say to me, "That's a very strong statement!"

Genesis 2:24 says: *"...a man shall leave his father and mother and cleave to his wife, and they shall become one flesh."*

It doesn't say that a man should 'cleave to his wife, his girlfriend or lover'. It simply says, *'cleave to his wife, and they shall become one...'* When we step out of the 'Devine Order', things do go dangerously wrong. Unwanted babies, sexually transmitted infections, broken marriages, divorce, domestic violence, abduction, rape, abuse and murder; these can all be the result of sexual activity outside of the confines of marriage. Not to mention grieving the heart of God!

Sexual abuse includes: voyeurism, indecent exposure, sexual harassment, molestation, sexual assault, violation, buggery, incest and rape. These are vile practices and again it is hard to imagine that such evils can take place within a family unit... yet they do. It is commonly accepted among law enforcement agencies that the vast proportion of these crimes, are perpetrated by family members.

Verbal, psychological and spiritual abuse involves domination, intimidation, and manipulation and it's not pleasant being under any of these forces. One still comes away from such experiences as though one has been used and in some way violated. While these practices may be 'perceived' as physically non-violent, they are, nevertheless, abuse. These practices can be just as terrifying, and may seriously damage the victim mentally and emotionally, in much the same way as physical and sexual abuse does.

Recently we have seen the rise of another form of abuse called on-line bullying which takes place on social media websites. Tragically, on–line bullying has resulted in several young people taking their own lives.

Each type of abuse can have a lasting effect upon the victims. Victims of abuse may suffer consequences which often seem to be totally unrelated, such as nightmares, flash-backs, bed-wetting, chronic depression, anxiety, post-traumatic stress, dissociation (the separation of mental processes, so that they lead an independent existence), anger, alcoholism, drug abuse, hyper-vigilance, intrusive imagery, avoidance behaviours, alexithymia (difficulty identifying and processing their own emotions), fear, comfort eating, bulimia, anorexia, self-harm, loss of identity and gynaecological problems in girls... and the list goes on. It is tragic that the innocent party or victim of abuse or rape can be led into sinful practices themselves.

People who perform acts of abuse appear not to realise the distress and damage they cause to their victims. Often they do not even recognise they are doing anything wrong. For some ridiculously perverse reason, many perpetrators of sexual abuse believe that their victims were fully consenting and even egged them on.

On a personal note: I was sexually abused as a

child and later as a teenager. They were two separate and totally unrelated incidents and my responses in both cases were very different. I was around seven years old when I was first abused by a woman. It wasn't a family member, I hasten to add, nor was it anyone I knew. At least I don't think it was since I didn't see her face; I was too frightened to look.

My defence mechanism, as a child, was to blot out its memory. I found no resolution to certain questions. I call these the 'unanswerable questions'. Such as: "To whom do I turn?", "This is something dirty, how can I talk to anyone?" "I've been a naughty boy; how can I tell mother?" "How can I speak about things I don't understand myself?" In this way the innocent child, exposed to an 'adult' world, has no means of handling it and is therefore silenced. In my case, not only was I silenced, I shut it down and blotted it out. Somehow I managed to erase the experience almost entirely from my memory... except from that point onwards, I had to live with certain unpleasant consequences. And there are always consequences.

The once happy-go-lucky seven year-old, without a care in the world, became serious, melancholic and introverted. I lost confidence and wet the bed. I feared being bathed. Bizarrely, I never allowed my parents to bath me after the abuse. I sometimes look back and wonder, "Why didn't they spot the signs?!" But of course people weren't sensitized to such things in the nineteen fifties.

I was afraid of the dark and feared someone lying under my bed like a monster ready to 'get me' when I fell asleep. I was afraid of taking a shower with fellow pupils after PE or swimming. I feared undressing in front of people. And a sense of rejection developed that has lingered throughout the majority of my adult life.

It wasn't until almost fifty years later that the memories slowly began to return. I'm grateful to God that the memories returned little by little; I don't think I could have handled it had they returned all at once. It was bad enough having the memories return in dribs and drabs let alone having them return in one go. There are still, to this day, aspects of my childhood abuse that I cannot remember, so I let those things go. I do not wrestle with them or hold on to them any longer. I think, "If I can't remember, it's better I don't remember". The important thing to me at this moment in time is that God knows. I look at it this way. God has made as much known to me as is necessary to bring me to a place of peace and acceptance. I can now put it all down to life and to experience. And that, I think, is a truly remarkable place to be. Perhaps 'remarkable' is too weak a word. Maybe *wonderful* is a far better label for it. Herein I am thankful.

The abuse I endured as a teenager was entirely different, for I remember almost every detail. I was sexually assaulted one day by a work colleague in the factory's outside toilet. There are three reactions that counsellors recognise in these situations; they are flight, fight and freeze. In my case, I froze.

Some might say, "Why didn't you shout?" or "Why didn't you thump him?" I couldn't… everything shut down; my strength deserted me and I had no means of fighting back. I wanted to shout… but no words came out of my mouth. I have heard it said that when a lion takes its prey, the antelope or zebra is momentarily paralysed by fear and feels no pain. I can't say that

I didn't feel mental or emotional pain... but I did go numb and was struck dumb!

Some women who are raped will put up one heck of a fight - shout, scream, kick, punch, scratch bite - while others will run. Still others will try to scream - but there is no sound. Everything shuts down, as I have said, and it is as though your very life and strength have departed like starlings in winter flight. Women who *flee* or *freeze* are in no way inferior to those who *fight*. None of us knows how we might react in such ignoble circumstances.

Personally speaking, I think that one of the vilest methods whereby many victims of sexual abuse are silenced is when the abuser says, "It's our little secret!" This is what my abuser said to me. Those four words form one of the most abominable phrases ever to be uttered by a human being (I think). That phrase takes hold of you, keeps you trapped and keeps you silenced. In the long term it can cause immense emotional suffering and mental anguish.

Coming to terms with abuse is difficult. It's not just the despicable deeds themselves that you have to come to terms with; it's also your own feelings – feelings of guilt, shame, self-blame, self-abasement and lack of self-worth. Then there are the feelings of anger, hatred and resentment that you feel towards the one who has harmed you, degraded you, defiled you and has stolen your innocence. In addition, there are those 'unanswerable questions' and the 'ifs and buts'.

The 'unanswerable questions' for me were: "*Why* did I choose to use that outside toilet?" "*Why* didn't I turn and run towards the lads working in the yard when I saw him following me?" "*Why* didn't I shout?"

"*Why* didn't I kick him in the unmentionables?" "*Why* did he do that to me?" "*What* on earth was he thinking?" The 'ifs' and 'buts' were: "*If* only I'd have gone to the loo five minutes earlier, it might never have happened!"; "*If* I tell, I'll be a snitch!"; "*If* I tell, I'll get into trouble and may even lose my job!"; "*But* I cannot tell, no one will believe me!"; "*But* I can't speak out for fear of retribution!"

There are no satisfactory answers to any of these questions and responses. The rehearsal of them in our mind only adds fuel to the fire of our anger, bitterness, resentment and hatred. Tragically, all we are doing is keeping ourselves locked in one vicious circle.

The only way forward is to begin to 'let go'. Whatever the 'unanswerable questions' are, and whatever the 'ifs' and 'buts' may be, you have to let them go. If you can't, then tell God. Tell Him you are struggling to let go and ask Him for help.

In addition, do not dismiss the idea of seeking specialist help, such as counselling or psychotherapy. You would visit a doctor or physiotherapist if you'd torn a muscle. So why not seek counselling or therapy with torn emotions? Our mind and our emotions are just as much a part of our body as our arms, legs and internal organs, as I have said before. So, what is the difference? My advice is, seek help; it's out there. It's confidential, it's discreet and, above all else, it can be very helpful.

Christian counselling and therapy are not going to put right the dreadful wrongs done nor change the events that have taken place. They will, however, help you come to terms with them, in order to get through and get on with the rest of your life.

Where Heaven Touches Earth

It is important that we come to terms with our abuse in the presence of God or else it may haunt us and cleave to us for the rest of our lives.

In the next story we will witness despicable acts performed by an adult upon a minor in his care. We see an adult who has deserted his responsibility, cast aside his own dignity and sunk to an unbelievable level of sin and degradation. But we shall also witness the love and the grace of God at work in the torn emotions of a broken life.

We do NOT have to stay trapped in a cycle of misery. There is a way through! There is a way out!

> *Dear Lord I'm hearing things that I don't really want to hear, but I know I need to hear them. The way ahead is frightening and the task too great for me on my own. Will You help me, lead me, guide me and bring me through to a place of healing and wholeness? In Jesus' name I ask, Amen. (Prayer written by Rob Giles 2014)*

22

Deborah's Story: Hope, Deliverance and Forgiveness

"…to comfort all who mourn, to console those who mourn in Zion, to give them beauty for ashes, the oil of joy for mourning, the garment of praise for the spirit of heaviness; that they may be called trees of righteousness, the planting of the Lord that He may be glorified." (Isaiah 61:2-3) "For I am persuaded that neither death nor life, nor angels nor principalities nor powers, nor things present nor things to come, nor height nor depth, nor any other created thing, shall be able to separate us from the love of God which is in Christ Jesus our Lord." (Romans 8:38&39)

Brought up in a dysfunctional family and abused by her stepfather from an early age, Deborah's life was one of secrets and lies, violent and abusive relationships, sex, drugs and heart-breaking tragedy. Her horrifying story and personal tragedy are contrasted by hope, deliverance and forgiveness, as God stepped into her seemingly lost cause and lost soul.

Deborah was around two to three years old when her mother and stepfather were married. It was a very up-and-down relationship and they were very poor. Her stepfather had come to Britain from Jamaica in the late nineteen fifties, no doubt seeking his fortune. He was a gambler and drinker, very domineering, manipulative and controlling. Bizarrely, he practised a form of witchcraft called *obea*. "That combination," said Deborah, "was very spiritual, but not in a good way; I'm convinced he had mental health problems."

From the early age of five he began to abuse her sexually and, in her own words, "My whole life was secrets and lies within the family. I remember when I was about seven, coming home from school one day. I was walking down the road and picking leaves and instead of saying 'He loves me, he loves me not' I said, 'He's going to die, he's not going to die, he's going to die, he's not going to die'; I really did wish him dead. My mom, on the other hand, was a very beautiful Christian woman but dominated by my stepfather. At weekends I'd go and stay with my grandmother, which was a welcome respite. I recall her saying to me more than once, 'If ever you are scared, just pray to Jesus.' I used to think, 'Jesus wouldn't help me; He's never helped me in the past, so why would He help me now?'"

"Even as a little girl, I had an aversion to Jesus. And anything relating to 'Heavenly Father' – Oh, my gosh! That would really freak me out! The worst thing anyone could say to me was 'Father' - it was something evil, something domineering and something controlling. Why would I want *Father* in my life?"

Continuing Deborah's harrowing story, "I was also

sexually abused by my uncle as a little child. What made matters worse, I was made to sit on his lap whenever he came to visit us or we visited him. I was unable to comprehend fully what was going on at the time. All I knew was that this was a bad, bad feeling - and I didn't like it. I was trying to get off his lap and he held me very tightly, while everyone said, 'Stop it; sit still on your uncle's lap.' I now have this thing with children; if I see someone trying to force them to sit on someone's lap when they don't want to, I say, 'Please don't do that to them; they should be able to choose.' I wish someone had done that for me... and given me the choice!!"

From the age of fourteen Deborah was forced to have full sex with her stepfather. Later she became pregnant by him and was pressed into having an abortion. Being a minor, the decision was not hers.

When asked about the abortion, Deborah replied, "It is an abominable sin: it is taking a precious God-given life."

Her stepfather concocted a deceptive plan of action. Deborah recalls, "I had to tell my mom I was pregnant and I had to make up a fictitious boyfriend. My stepfather told me exactly what to say and what to do... so I went to my mom's work and told her. Later at home, when mom told him that I was pregnant, to my surprise he 'hit the roof'. He went absolutely ballistic. After that, there was a lot of domestic violence. He used to beat my mom and we all lived in fear of our lives. I don't think my mom had any idea of what really went on; I have always believed she never knew the real truth."

"When I had the abortion and was in hospital, I still

didn't fully understand; I was very naive. I somehow knew I had been sexually abused, but I had this crazy notion that because it was such a secret, maybe this sort of stuff was the norm and happening everywhere!! My stepfather used to threaten me by saying, 'No one will believe you. And if you say anything I will have to kill you and your mom... and it will be your fault,' and I believed him!"

"Our home life was like the 'Fred West' story, (British serial killer, rapist and child molester) the only difference being there were no deaths - no one actually got killed. You see, I could relate to the stories of the children who were abused there. When I hear folk say, 'Why on earth didn't they speak out?', I understand. It was fear... fear of what might happen and fear of reprisals. Fear grips you and you become trapped. You think you are to blame. You think that no one will believe you, and so you become defensive. You don't want to build real relationships and if someone gets too close, you put up defences. I felt as though the world *owed* me. I hated the world and the world hated me. That's how I felt. One sin leads to another and before you know it"

As soon as she was sixteen, Deborah left home. One day, however, she went back to the house to collect some of her things. Deborah picks up the story:

"My little sister let me in, but my stepfather phoned the police and had me arrested for unlawful entry. He said he would drop the charges if I came back home... I refused. And so I was arrested, charged and ended up with a criminal record."

Throughout this devastating period she still couldn't bring herself to talk about the horrors of what had taken place. "I didn't tell anyone... I felt so ashamed! It was entirely my fault! No one else was to blame! I thought to myself, 'There must be something wrong with me! Why else would this be happening?'"

All that had taken place had a dramatic affect upon her relationships with boyfriends and partners. "I just thought that sex was what men wanted!" she said. "In any case, I never felt that I was worthy of love and affection."

When Deborah left home she was rebellious (to say the least). To use her own words, "I was anti everything, anti establishment... anti God. There was no God to me! Having said that, though, there was always something niggling at the back of my mind...there was something missing in my life and I wondered what it was. I was always looking for that elusive *something*."

She went through a series of relationships that were very violent and abusive before meeting a fellow she refers to as 'JB'. Affectionately, she said of him, "He was wonderful...he was such a lovely, lovely man." They had a daughter together named Melissa, "A beautiful gift", as Deborah put it. But when the child was sixteen months old, tragedy struck. She was taken into hospital for an operation on what was thought to be a blockage of the bowel. However, it turned out to be peritonitis... her appendix had ruptured. She later died with Deborah by her bedside.

In the next bed was a child who, allegedly, had been physically abused by its parents. The child had apparently been thrown down the stairs but survived. The mother was arrested at the bedside while Deborah looked on. "I became so angry", she said. "I shouted out 'How can anyone say there is a God? A child that

Where Heaven Touches Earth

isn't wanted lives, while mine who *is* wanted dies! It isn't fair!"

Instead of turning to God she turned away and sank further into sin.

"When Melissa died, it broke my heart. I had taken drugs in the past but after that incident I'd take anything and everything that was available to me. I was pushing boundaries all the time. I was pushing JB, pushing and pushing him all the time. I was so 'coked' up, I wanted to die; I just couldn't see any future. I was really horrible to JB, and probably because I was so damaged, I pushed him away. Then, of course, we split up."

What followed was a string of relationships that were again violent. Then she met the man she married, the man who became the father of her son. Deborah spoke affectionately of her son's father. "He was a lovely man, he was very generous and he never ever hurt me."

"But he too was heavily into drugs and was also a dealer. He had another major problem… women! He couldn't say *no* to a woman. He even admitted that women were his biggest weakness. I just could not cope… I wanted him to stop. I wanted him to stop selling drugs and I wanted him to change… It was then that I recognised, possibly for the first time, you can only change if you really want to. I felt I had no choice but to leave him for the safety of my child. So I left him and went into a women's refuge and that's where my life began to change."

While Deborah was in residence at the refuge, she met a Christian lady, Penny, who worked there. Penny turned out to be a great source of encouragement and a good friend. She was the one who bought Deborah her very first Bible.

"She was lovely to me and I found it difficult to understand why she was so nice; I hadn't received this kind of attention before. She always listened, never asked loads of questions and never pushed and probed for answers even though I didn't tell her my story. I used to write poetry, and her comments were so encouraging to me. Once, when she had read one of my poems, she said to me, 'You've got a real gift... Why not come to my house on Sunday for a meal? Perhaps we'll go to Church first?' I thought to myself, 'Oh well, if she wants to take me and my son for a free meal, then that's fine'."

"One Sunday, she took me and my son along to the Church. It was a lively Pentecostal gathering. They used to clap and wave their hands in the air. I stood there thinking, 'Oh my! Crazy or what? You'd never get me doing anything like that.' However, if I was ever going to find Jesus, it would be because somebody cared about me and that someone had actually taken an interest in me. Penny was that person. She saw in me something no one else had seen... that made me feel special."

"The pastor was preaching one Sunday. I didn't know him, he didn't know me neither did he know anything about my story. That morning he happened to be speaking about the community and damaged people. In the middle of his sermon he stopped, looked straight at me and pointed. 'You know what I am talking about don't you?' As he said those words, I slid to my knees. The most wonderful feeling I've ever experienced came over me; it was like a 'rush' that went straight through me."

Where Heaven Touches Earth

"Penny turned to me and said, 'Deborah, are you OK?' 'Yeah, I'm fine; I've just had this amazing feeling like nothing I've ever had before!' 'What?' she exclaimed. I looked at her and said, 'I want to follow Jesus'. 'Are you sure… do you want to think about it?' 'No… I want this feeling all the time; I don't want it to go away.'"

"I had never felt like this in all my life - happiness, joy, peace; I didn't want it to go away. I felt ten feet tall! It was truly one of those Holy Spirit moments one experiences from time to time. After the service, Penny went and found a lady named Sylvia and together they prayed with me. I told them, 'I want to become a Christian', and so they took me into a back room to pray more privately."

"I remember going home that night and preparing to do my ironing. I'll never forget it. I was singing and then I just dropped to my knees and began to cry. They weren't tears of sadness, but tears of joy. I felt so happy all my sins had gone. I felt so free. I was worshipping and praising God out loud, 'Oh Jesus, I love you! Jesus I love you!' The words just flowed out of my mouth and I sobbed, and sobbed and sobbed. Two weeks later I was baptised!"

"Before the baptism, the pastor asked me if I had got a little speech ready. I remember saying to him, 'I'm saying nothing in front of this lot.' He said to me, 'I think you should at least say that you love Jesus.' 'Alright,' I replied, 'I'll say that.' There were several being baptised that Sunday, and when he came to me and handed me the microphone, oh boy, I couldn't shut up! I must have gone on for twenty to thirty minutes as I told my story. I scared myself, because I finished by telling them about the love of God and how they should be beacons of light going out into the community. I said, 'There's an estate over the road, you should be there loving people. There are poor people out there, just like me, who need Jesus.'"

Deborah's life changed from that point on as she moved away from her sinful life of drugs and sex. It changed dramatically in a very short space of time. Formerly, she had laughed at those who raised their hands in worship, saying, 'Oh my gosh! Crazy or what? You'd never get me doing anything like that.' Now, however, she was doing the very same thing! She laughed and said, "I never thought I'd become one of those Jesus-freaks!"

Some of the important changes wrought in her life were things such as taking part in discipleship training at the Church and enrolling for a college course. The former was beneficial for her spiritual growth and the latter played a major role in acquiring formal qualifications. Deborah hadn't performed at all well at school. Although intelligent, her behaviour had let her down badly. "All I now knew was - I loved Jesus... I didn't care too much about anything else; I just wanted to follow Christ."

But it was counselling, and the subsequent outcome, that had the greatest impact upon Deborah's life. She took part in counselling sessions at a place called The Well. In those days, The Well was a vibrant place with a strong, sensitive counselling team. The female staff helped her come to terms with the abuse she'd suffered during her childhood and early teens. They also helped her in coming to terms with the abortion, which she was forced to have as a minor.

Where Heaven Touches Earth

Deborah said once more of the abortion, "It is an abominable sin: it is taking a precious God given life."

There in the counselling room, she was able to repent of the part she had played in taking that 'precious life' in the abortion. She was able too, to repent of her sinful life of immorality and drug abuse. It was there she received forgiveness from God.

She said of the Christian counsellors at The Well, "They were absolutely fantastic, the way they dealt with me, prayed with me and led me to Jesus. Looking back, I'm so grateful to them for helping me bring all the horrors of my life to the feet of Jesus and to see all my sins nailed to the cross."

"There were no limits placed upon the number of consultations needed. They were there for me as long as it took. I actually went to The Well for over a year."

"When I first visited The Well, I was unable to say my stepfather's name and even to speak my uncle's name; I just called them my abusers. My counsellor said to me, 'I believe that by the end you will be able to face your abuser.' That I found to be a little scary, to say the least; nevertheless, I persevered with each session, week by week. Eventually, I was able to re-live everything with my counsellor in the counselling room. They bathed me in prayer; there was so much love and understanding..."

"Towards the end of my time at The Well, I asked my counsellor, 'When will it be okay to stop coming?' 'When you can actually forgive and move on; that's when the real freedom will come.' 'Oh, I'll never forgive,' I said, 'no way on this earth. I cannot forgive because that would be like saying everything is alright.' I now know that isn't true."

"Around the same time, my son and I went to stay with my brother for a brief while. My mother's home was only a short walk from my brother's and one Sunday morning I made a spur-of-the-moment decision to visit her. I said to my brother, 'I'm going to pay Mom a visit; will you look after my son for me while I'm gone? I won't be away many minutes.' He readily agreed, so off I went."

"When I arrived, my stepfather was sitting in the front room. I said nothing but went straight into the kitchen to give my mom a big hug. I said, 'I love you loads. But I may not come back again... well not after today.' 'Why's that?' 'I don't really know how things will work out after today.' I then went into the front room and *he* was sitting there in his big leather chair. He was a big man, well over six feet tall, but suddenly, he seemed so small. I felt sorry for him, and bizarrely, I felt a lot of love in my heart for him at that moment. I stared at him and said, 'I've only come to say I forgive you for what you did to me.' 'I didn't do anything', he replied. 'Oh yes, you did!' I said, 'you abused me! You made my life a misery! But I just want to tell you, I forgive you'. He kept saying to me, 'I never did anything! I never did anything!' Then he stopped abruptly and scowled, 'Get out of my house!'"

"At that point he looked really weak. As I gazed at him I felt even more sorry for him than before. 'I am not going to let you have any control over me ever again,' I told him emphatically, 'I forgive you! If you want to accept it, that is entirely up to you, but you will have no control over me any more. Jesus loves you!' His exact words were like a hissing serpent, 'My god is bigger than your God.' 'No!' I replied, 'my God is much stronger than your god and He loves you very much.' 'Get out my house!' he yelled at me, 'get out my house!' 'OK, I will,' and with that I walked out."

"When I stepped outside I felt free. It was as if my feet weren't touching the floor. I felt as though I was floating on air. There was a peace upon me. There was a peace in my heart that was indescribable. It was peace, it was joy, it was freedom all rolled into one; and for the first time in my life I felt completely free!"

"Upon returning to my brother's house, he just stared at me nonplussed, 'Are you OK? You're shining… you look really happy.' 'Yes I am - really happy.' 'What's happened?' 'Oh nothing's happened; I've just been to see Mom.' I felt it was unnecessary to explain but from that day to this, I've known the power of forgiveness. I can honestly say it has brought complete freedom. It's not weakness to forgive; it is strength. It's a strength that brings liberation. When we are bitter and angry with those who have harmed us, we are actually allowing the powers of darkness to have sway over our lives. The only way to combat those evil forces is by love and forgiveness. Love will pierce the darkness and forgiveness will bring emancipation. When we forgive, we're not saying that what that person did to us is OK. On the contrary, when we forgive we're proclaiming to the powers of darkness, 'You have no hold over me any longer.' The only way forward is to forgive."

Deborah's stepfather, mother and uncle have all passed away. Recently her husband died of cancer. She now lives with her son and uses her maiden name. She remains unmarried.

Deborah runs a community project in the UK, well thought of by the Borough in which she lives and has recently received an award from the Queen for her efforts in the community. Ironically, the community project is situated just over the way from the Church where she was baptised - where she had said to the congregation, 'There's an estate over the road; you should be there loving people. There are poor people out there, just like me, who need Jesus.' Those poor people, just like her, are the very ones she now serves. Congratulations to her for the award she and the project have received.

Dear Lord, I praise You for Your amazing grace. I thank You that no one can fall so low they cannot be reached by Your love. Touch my heart with the heavenly fire of the Holy Spirit, O God. May my life be transformed to become a vessel of honour, bringing glory, praise and pleasure to You, in the name of Jesus. Amen. (Prayer written by Rob Giles 2014)

23

A Question of Resentment

"Now Joseph had a dream, and he told it to his brothers; and they hated him even more. (Genesis 37:5) "And forgive us our sins, for we also forgive everyone who is indebted to us..." (Luke 11:4)

Most of us will feel a degree of resentment at some stage in our lives. More often than not we experience it in minor annoyances. "Are you really going to mow the lawn today?" says the wife to her husband for the umpteenth time, "How many times do I have to ask!?" Or the wife who is asked repeatedly by her husband, "Have you ironed my shirts yet? You know I need them for the golfing weekend!" It's annoying, but the resentment we feel is but fleeting and easily shaken off. We simply mutter something under our breath and move on before it settles in our mind. Sometimes, however, resentment is not so easily shaken off.

Resentment may develop through envy. For example, we might feel a little envious when a neighbour appears to get everything he (or she) desires while we struggle to make ends meet. After a while, by allowing it to *stew* in our mind, we may begin to resent our neighbour and their every purchase.

Resentment may develop when we allow anger to *simmer*. Resentment often derives from the anger we feel when we are badly hurt, either actual or perceived. The overwhelming sense of injustice causes indignation to *bubble* and *boil*; consequently, we begin to resent the person or persons who occasioned the hurt.

Resentment too may develop through rejection. If we are rejected and it appears blatant, we might feel an awful stab of hurt. For example, if we are 'passed over' for promotion, the experience has the potential to transform our sense of rejection or hurt into resentment.

The Twelve Steps manual says of resentment:

"Resentment is the bitterness and anger we feel toward those whom we perceive as threats to our security or well-being or those who have caused us harm. If not removed, our resentments hinder our progress and growth." (35)

We may think that Deborah had just reason to resent her stepfather in the light of what he did to her. It is easy to become embittered about the way we've been treated and it's easy to resent the persons involved. When we are embittered and resentful, however, it is very difficult to bring a halt to those feelings and emotions. Mistakenly, we think that resentment is caused by the horrid experiences we went through but it's not entirely the case. Neither is it caused solely by the individual who has occasioned the hurt. Resentment is caused by the *replaying* of the event, over and over in our mind, and by continually mulling over the injustice we feel. The sense of hurt we feel, fuelled by anger, soon *festers* and turns to resentment. Resentment settles and sticks. The more we nurse it, the more it grows; the more it grows, the more we nurse it. Resentment is *intoxicating*. The Collins Dictionary's definition of 'intoxicate' is *to stimulate and excite to the point where it overwhelms*. So we could say resentment *stimulates* to the point where the wrongs done become *overwhelming*.

Jesus told a parable, commonly called the Parable of the Unforgiving Servant. It is a powerful and tragic story. Jesus told the story to convey His teaching on forgiveness and He also told it to reveal what takes place in reality if we cannot *let go* of our resentments. Jesus uttered these chilling words:

"'...I forgave you all that debt because you begged me. Should you not also have had compassion on your fellow servant, just as I had pity on you?' And his master was angry, and delivered him to the torturers until he should pay all that was due to him." (Matthew 18:32-34)

"Are we tortured if we cannot let go of our resentments?" You bet your life we are! No one *actually* comes along to torture us; we do it ourselves! We torture ourselves relentlessly by replaying both event and aftermath over and over in our head.

Often we resent people who have harmed us because we want to get even, or in some way make them suffer. "I'll never forgive him for what he has done!" or "I won't ever trust a woman again!" or "I won't give them the time of day!" But we never seem to get the true justice we desire because resentment turns in on us and begins to eat us away, while the *villain* appears to walk free. Resentment is *toxic*. St Augustine said, *"Resentment is like taking poison and hoping the other person dies."* [36]

You might ask the question, "How then, do we stop harbouring our resentments?" There is only one way and that is to begin the process of 'letting go'.

Letting go is vital. Imagine you are on the upper floor of a building on fire. You step out onto the window sill and look down; your head begins to swim, you feel sick in your stomach, so you cling to the window frame for dear life. A friendly voice says, "Let go, I've got you." But you can't!! The fire fighter, however, is ready to take you over his shoulder to safety, but he can't... not until *you* let go!

Likewise, the same applies to resentment; letting go is crucial for you to come through to freedom. Letting go is the first step to peace, wholeness and healing.

The *letting go* process will probably be one of the toughest things you will ever do, for there will never be a convenient moment to begin that process. There will never seem to be a moment when your mind is free enough to begin. Be that as it may, you have to start somewhere. For me, it began with slowly shutting down the thoughts that added fuel to the fire of my resentment, such as, "What a dastardly thing to do!" or "What a swine!" Instead, I began thinking to myself, "No! I'm not going to think this way!" Gradually, with the help of God in quiet prayer, I began to let go of *questions* that fed my resentment.

Had I kept replaying in mind and thinking to myself, "What a dastardly deed!" or "You swine"... I'd still be resentful now. It is painful to let go, because there will always be those 'unanswerable questions', those 'ifs' and 'buts' swirling around in your head but you must not listen to them. Should you continue to listen, resentment will begin its corrosive work like acid eating its way through a tin pot.

Letting go is not a gift to the person you resent, it is a gift to you. Because you are not hurting them you are hurting yourself.

Letting go is never easy so I say again you may need to seek help, such as counselling or psychotherapy. Don't dismiss specialist help. You must, one way or another, get through your resentments for your own peace of mind, for your own well-being and for your own sanity. We don't have control over the events that have happened in our past, but we do have a *strong* say over what role those events might play in our present. So put an end to the torture.

> *Dear Lord Jesus, now I'm beginning to see what resentment is doing to me. This is too big an issue for me to handle on my own. Will You help me? Will You walk with me through this painful journey? Because right now I don't think I can forgive. I know that You forgave me as they drove the nails into Your hands and feet, so come, dear Lord and fill me - with Your love and supernatural power. In Jesus' name, Amen! (Prayer written by Rob Giles 2014)*

24

Praying with Forgiveness

"You have heard that it was said, 'You shall love your neighbour and hate your enemy'. But I say to you, love your enemies, bless those who curse you, do good to those who hate you, and pray for those who spitefully use you and persecute you, that you may be sons of your Father in heaven..." (Matthew 5:43-45) "And forgive us our sins, for we also forgive everyone who is indebted to us..." (Luke 11:4) "For if you forgive men their trespasses, your heavenly Father will also forgive you. But if you do not forgive men their trespasses, neither will your Father forgive your trespasses." (Matthew 6:14&15)

What is praying with forgiveness? Praying with forgiveness is praying for those who badly use us, and forgiving those who have 'hacked' us off or rubbed us up the wrong way. It is praying for, and forgiving, those who have pulled out in front of us while we're driving. It is praying for, and forgiving, those who have given us the 'V' sign when we've made a simple error. It is praying for, and forgiving, those who have wronged us, hurt us or have caused us harm. That last sentence may prove difficult for many, particularly for those who have been seriously harmed or damaged; I accept that. Nevertheless, praying for those who despise us and forgiving those who have hurt us are pure Christian responses. Deborah discovered this firsthand when she walked into the lounge and forgave her stepfather to his face. It *was* a pure response; and that response began to change the whole of her life, little by little.

We don't have to look very far to discover the Biblical basis of forgiveness; we come face to face with it at the cross. There we see the Lord Jesus praying as they drove the nails into his hands, *"...Father, forgive them, for they do not know what they do..." (Luke 23:34).* This is the crux of the Christian faith. God unreservedly forgives all who come to Him in repentance and faith in Jesus Christ. And we, you and I that is, are called to follow in the steps of the Master and do as He has done. *"For to this you were called, because Christ also suffered for us, leaving us an example, that you should follow in his steps." (1Peter 2:21)* This is a truly high calling.

On one occasion the Apostle Peter came to Jesus and asked a searching question. I imagine it's a question all of us may have asked, or at least thought about, at some stage, in grappling with forgiveness:

"'...Lord, how often shall my brother sin against me, and I forgive him? Up to seven times?' Jesus said to him, 'I do not say to you, up to seven times, but up to seventy times seven.'"(Matthew 18:21&22)

Jesus didn't slip in a clause that gives us a little leeway depending upon the severity of our mistreatment. On the contrary, He said emphatically, *"I do not say to you, (forgive) up to seven times, but up to seventy times seven."*

Then, continuing with His answer, He told the story of the Unforgiving Servant. In conclusion, Jesus said these words, *"'...I forgave you all that debt because you begged me. Should you not also have had compassion on your fellow servant, just as I had pity on you?'" (Matthew 18:32-33)*

The message that Christ sought to convey to us can be in no doubt; God has freely forgiven our debt of sin... we therefore should forgive others. This is the *absolute* in terms of Christian living... this is the bottom line in terms of Christian responses... but often, in reality, we are a long, long way from embracing this particular truth.

Many of us will know the story of Stephen (see Acts 7) - how he was falsely accused, arrested and executed by being stoned. Now, we can easily gloss over this barbaric act when we read the story in the Bible because it doesn't go into graphic detail. But stoning was a wild, violent, frenzied affair. Those who threw the stones (and these were not pebbles) were hyped up and psyched up. They threw the stones with merciless intent, venom and hatred. At some stage of the slaughter, most likely when the victim had fallen to the ground, they would stand over him (or her) and smash stones the size of house bricks over the head and body with mocking taunts, calling down curses and shouting obscenities.

However, those who are familiar with Stephen's story will no doubt recall that with his dying breath he prayed with a loud voice, *"...Lord, do not charge them with this sin..."(Acts 7:60)* In other words, Stephen was not only forgiving those who were taking his life but he was requesting God to forgive likewise!

Now I've deliberately written up the startling details of stoning to show the magnitude of Stephen's forgiving heart. Stephen was *truly* following in the steps of Christ and doing as He had done... suffering with fortitude and forgiving from the heart.

Forgiveness, as we all know, is central to the Lord's Prayer. Right in the middle of the prayer we find these words, *"...and forgive us our trespasses as we forgive those who trespass against us."* This line is repeated in every school or Church service where the Lord's Prayer is recited. Forgiveness is a two-way act; we ask God to forgive us - and we forgive those who have wronged us. We cannot run away from forgiveness.

The Apostle Paul taught forgiveness in his letters; *"And be kind to one another, tenderhearted, forgiving one another, even as God in Christ forgave you." (Ephesians 4:32)* and again, *"Bearing with one another, and forgiving one another, if anyone has a complaint against another; even as Christ forgave you, so you also must do." (Colossians 3:13)* Forgiveness is not a complete *entity*, until it is given away.

You might say, "Why entity?" I say *entity* because forgiveness, like entity, is *"something real and having distinct existence."* [37] And Christ Himself, of course, is the living embodiment of forgiveness.

Forgiveness may raise several questions in the minds of those who have been badly hurt or seriously damaged. "Does this mean that you forget what has happened?" Certainly not! Those who have forgiven do not forget the horrifying events... but the awful pain of resentment and the soul-destroying hatred are taken away when we forgive. "If I forgive, am I justifying what that person has done to me?" or "If I forgive, am

I excusing their behaviour?" No, not at all! They have still committed the offence... that does not alter. But you are freeing yourself from unhelpful, unnecessary pain and torture. "If I forgive, am I letting those who have harmed me off the hook?" No you're not! You are letting yourself off the hook, for the only person who is hurting in all of this is *you* - no one else. Those who have harmed you may not have any concept of the pain they have caused. But God knows and He is working with you and for you.

Letting go relates to the unanswerable questions and the 'ifs' and 'buts', as we have already seen. Releasing is another step in the process of forgiving. In this instance it relates to *releasing* the perpetrator from your heart and mind. This we do by releasing that person to God. This we do with a prayerful heart. It will more than likely be something you will have to do over and over before you are able to fully forgive from the heart. This was true in my experience of forgiving.

Prayer is a powerful tool; we must not underestimate its potential. We should use it. Tell God everything; tell God what you can and cannot do.

Prayer is the *best* place to be when we forgive.

Jesus was in prayer when he forgave from the cross. Stephen was in prayer when he forgave as he breathed his last. As we have already said, Jesus taught us to pray and to forgive in what we call the Lord's Prayer.

Prayer is the *safest* place to be when we forgive.

When we forgive there may be an element of opening of old wounds. And speaking metaphorically, those wounds will no doubt be infected with bitterness and resentment. The conscious presence of God is by far the safest place to be when opening old wounds.

Where Heaven Touches Earth

We may be certain of this one thing: God has our best interests at heart. He is on our side and He is working with us to effect change, healing and wholeness in every aspect of our lives. Prayer is by far the *safest* place to be when we forgive.

Prayer is the *easiest* place to forgive.

Don't get me wrong. I am not saying that it is 'easy' to forgive - on the contrary. I'm simply stating that it is *easier* to forgive while we are in prayer. If we are ever going to let go, release and forgive, the *conscious presence* of God will be by far the easiest place to be. The journey from hatred, anger, bitterness and resentment to forgiveness may prove to be a long and arduous process but it will be greatly *eased* through prayer. Prayer is by far the *easiest* place to forgive.

I have found the following steps to be particularly helpful.

Prayerfully introduce forgiveness into your life.

Begin introducing forgiveness in small ways. Forgive those who have 'hacked' you off or rubbed you up the wrong way. Forgive those who have pulled out in front of you while you are driving and forgive those who may have given you the 'V' sign when you have made a simple error. These are but small things, but forgiveness is powerful. Once forgiveness is allowed into your life-style, in terms of *giving it away*, it will grow (no matter how small those acts of forgiveness are). And once you begin to forgive, forgiveness will change your demeanour, your character, your life.

Pray for others.

Pray for those who are struggling with resentment and wrestling with comparable issues to yours. You are ideally positioned to pray for someone in a similar predicament, for you know what it's like to suffer in that particular way. Praying in this fashion is a powerful means of prayer, because you are actually turning away from *self* (which is important), and you are deliberately thinking about someone else (which is vital). This is the way of Christ. He prayed for us while He suffered in agony on the cross. When you pray this way you are fulfilling the Word of God that says: *"... whatever a man sows, that he will also reap" (Galatians 6:7)* and *"...whatever you want men to do to you, do also to them..." (Matthew 7:12)*.

Pray in contemplation.

Contemplative prayer can be of great value in the forgiving process, for the whole essence of contemplative prayer is, as we have seen, one of stillness, letting go, releasing, worship and peace. These are the appropriate responses, the tools needed in drawing near to God and progressing down the road of recovery through forgiveness.

Prayerfully explore picture-imaging.

This step involves, prayerfully forming a mental picture of what you want to achieve and then visualizing yourself actually performing it. I pictured myself taking my alcoholism, loosening my grip and giving it to God. I then pictured Jesus taking that burden away. I performed *picture-imaging* often, whenever my problem was at the forefront of my mind. I actually did this consistently over a period of thirteen months, while working with God to see my addiction to alcohol broken. The contemplative way is never to worry and never to panic - but to be quiet. Then, keep bringing it to God – keep believing – keep laying it down - until it breaks. If you want radical *picture-imagery*, envisage

Where Heaven Touches Earth

laying the habit on the altar and God consuming it with Holy Fire.

In addition, I often asked the Lord to show me if there were any obstacles or hindrances preventing me from letting go. So I sometimes used this prayer of David, *"Search me, O God, and know my heart; try me, and know my anxieties; and see if there is any wicked way in me, and lead me in the way everlasting." (Psalm 139:23&24)* God, of course, knows what prevents us from actually *letting go* in reality – I believe He *will* reveal those things to us if we allow Him. During my thirteen months of struggle, God gradually revealed to me, one by one, the things that held me back from walking free of alcoholism.

The biggest hindrance to my recovery, would you believe, was the sexual abuse I'd suffered! I was shocked when God revealed this to me. I had no idea there was a connection between the sexual abuse I'd endured in my early years and the addiction to alcohol that I now battled. Somehow, miraculously, God brought me to the place where I was able to forgive my abusers from the heart, in prayer. When I forgave in prayer, it was so liberating. It was as though a great weight had been lifted off my shoulders… what's more, in a matter of weeks I was able to walk free from my alcohol addiction.

There is one point that needs to be made here. When I speak of walking free from alcohol addiction I am talking about repentance which leads to freedom in Christ. Repentance is far mote than confession of sin, as we have seen.

Forgiveness is a powerful *entity*.

The only way to put an end to the torture of

resentment is to forgive from the heart. Will you give it a try? Will you begin the process of letting go? Letting go is an amazing gift to your own heart. Above everything else – it works!

Heavenly Father, I give You my broken, tortured life. Unravel the mess and lead me to the place of peace. Teach me Your way, O God, and enable me to forgive from the heart… in reality… and in truth. I crave intimacy with You so, dear Father in Heaven, clear the way and pave the way, in Jesus' name, Amen. (Prayer written by Rob Giles 2014)

25

Acceptance: The Pathway to Peace

"Therefore, having been justified by faith, we have peace with God through our Lord Jesus Christ" (Romans 5:1). "Peace I leave with you, my peace I give to you; not as the world gives do I give to you. Let not your heart be troubled, neither let it be afraid." (John 14:27) "These things I have spoken to you, that in me you might have peace. In the world you will have tribulation; but be of good cheer, I have overcome the world." (John 16:33)

The Collins Dictionary and Thesaurus defines peace as *the state existing during the absence of war.* [38] This can be said to be true in our personal lives. We experience peace of mind in the absence of mental conflict and anxiety. We experience peace, emotionally, when emotional hostilities have ceased.

The Greek word used for *peace* in the above opening verses is *eirene*: pronounced phonetically, eye-ray-nay. It means: *"A state of rest, quietness and calmness; an absence of strife; tranquillity. It generally denotes a perfect well-being."* [39]

Peace is something all of us desire, be it peace of mind, a stress-free environment or relief from anxiety. I think the greatest aspect of peace from the above definition is *tranquillity*. Tranquillity is a constant, moment-by-moment, peaceful state. And those who live in tranquillity are at peace with God, at peace with themselves, at peace with their surroundings and at peace with their lot. To be able to walk through life in tranquillity is a wonderful gift... a great God-given gift. We may have met one or two such people in our lifetime and I guess we've wondered, 'What is their secret?' Now I use the word 'secret', because to live in tranquillity is certainly not the norm in our modern world. But I believe we can.

Philippians 4:7 of The Amplified Bible says, *"And God's peace [shall be yours, that tranquil state of a soul assured of its salvation through Christ, and so fearing nothing from God and being content with its earthly lot of whatever sort that is, that peace] which transcends all understanding shall garrison and mount guard over your hearts and minds in Christ Jesus."*

This verse sums up exactly what we have been talking about.

Peace is something of a conundrum. Peace does not depend upon our circumstances. If it did, from time to time, we would need our circumstances to change. Yet, while peace occurs in the absence of striving, anxiety, mental conflict and emotional strife, it doesn't mean we cannot find peace in the midst of those difficulties. You may be wondering, "Is it really possible to be at peace, live at peace and walk in peace amidst the pressures of general living?" In answer to that question, listen to the words of Jesus: *"These things I have spoken to you, that in me you might have peace. In the world you will have tribulation; but be of good cheer, I have overcome the world."* (John 16:33)

Returning to Philippians 4:7 for one moment, Paul says: "That peace, which transcends all understanding, shall garrison and mount guard over your hearts and minds..." The Greek word translated as 'guard', is *phroureo*, pronounced phonetically froo-reh-oh. Strong says of its meaning... it is, *"a military term picturing a sentry standing guard as protection against the enemy. We are in spiritual combat, but God's power and peace are our sentinels and protectors."* [40] This is the kind of peace we need to meet life's tribulations... a peace that will 'garrison and mount guard' over our hearts and minds.

In life there are many things we cannot change. For instance, a bereaved person cannot change what has taken place, although they would dearly love to. He or she has to work through the grieving process, however long that process might be. They have to work through that process to arrive at a place of *acceptance*, in order to come to terms with their loss. Otherwise there can be no peace of mind for there will always be something in the back of their minds disturbing or hindering peace i.e. the tranquil state.

Likewise, people who have been abused cannot alter what has taken place in their lives. They must come to a place where they are able to let go of its crippling hold and accept what they cannot change.

Those who have worked through their grief, sorrow, pain and heartache, and have come to a place of acceptance, will discover that the strivings have ceased, the *war is over...* for acceptance is the path of peace.

Having acknowledged there are many things we cannot change, there are things in our lives that we *can* do something to change or, indeed, work with God to change. For example, changes from bad to good, wrong to right and from sinful to pleasing God. We can play a major role in changing attitudes such as: selfishness, bitterness, resentment, thanklessness, grumbling and lack of love. It will take courage, self-denial, strength of character and a repentant heart to do so but we *can* begin that process of change.

For many years the notions, "You mustn't do things in your 'own strength'" and "It's not by 'works of righteousness'" prevented me from stepping into the kind of freedom we have been talking about. I would still be praying now... 'Lord, make me thankful', had I not seized the initiative by thinking to myself. 'I'm going to be thankful anyway'. So I began thanking God for everyday mundane things. Slowly it **changed my life.** And into the bargain, I reaped other benefits besides a thankful heart.

We need to take the first step. Just as a car is easier to steer when it is moving, likewise, once we are prayerfully on the move, God is able to steer us in the right direction. If we take one step, God will take two to meet us.

You might ask, "So, is this 'works'?" No it's not 'works'. It's called 'cooperating with God'. It is simply working with God to see bad habits broken. I'm speaking here of making *simple* changes and taking *simple,* positive steps to go deeper with God in terms of our behaviour. I think this is all the more reason why we should embrace the quiet way of 'contemplation prayer' in order to pursue the paths leading to *contentment* and *peace*. The result will be moving from religion to relationship, and moving from religious acquaintance to intimacy with God.

All that is necessary is a quiet, prayerful heart and the peace that God alone can give in order to accept the things we cannot change. All we need is a quiet, prayerful, repentant heart, the will, the courage and the determination to work with God to see aspects of our lives changed for the better. Are we up for such a challenge?

Christ is longing to step into your grief, sorrow, pain and heartache. Will you allow him? Metaphorically speaking, the hand from heaven is reaching down to touch you. Will you respond by taking the Master's hand?

> *Lord God, You have enlightened my spirit and there is much food here for thought. Help me to process what I have read and grant me the grace, and the discernment to press forward with You by my side. I do not want to stay as I am for the rest of my life. Many of the virtues I've read about in this book are the very things I have longed for. Give me the desire to search the Scriptures to check their authenticity. Give me the will and the courage to cooperate with the Holy Spirit to make my behavioural aspirations a living reality. Help me, dear Lord, neither to miss nor dismiss the truth because it may seem unpalatable, for that would indeed be tragic… Amen. (Prayer written by Rob Giles 2014)*

REFERENCES

3

(1) *The Collins English Dictionary and Thesaurus*
(2) *Lexiconcordance.com/greek/3340.html*
(3) *The Amplified Bible, Expanded Edition, page 53, Copyright © 1987 by The Zondervan Corporation and the Lockman foundation, Zondervan Bible Publishers Grand Rapids Michigan, 1987*

4

(4) *Cited by Joni Eareckson Tada, Seeking God, page 53, Word Publishing Milton Keynes, England 1991*
(5) *Matthew Henry, Commentary on the Whole Bible in One Volume,' page 278, Marshal Morgan & Scott, London*
(6) *Oxford Quick Reference Dictionary, page 441*

6

(7) *Strong's #4286 Spirit Filled Life Bible, page 1701, Thomas Nelson Publishers, Nashville*
(8) *Tim Hughes, Everything, from the album, 'Holding Nothing Back', 2007, Survivor Records*

8

[9] Trevor Dearing, *Meditate And Be Made Whole Through Jesus Christ*, p.3, Crossbridge Books 2009

10

[10] Strong, #1826, *Strong's Concordance, Hebrew Dictionary (Lexicon-Concordance)*

[11] Jeanne Guyon, *Experiencing the Depths of Jesus Christ*, page 93, SeedSowers Publishing P.O. Box3317 Jacksonville, Florida., No publication date

[12] Strong's #3309 *Spirit Filled Life Bible*, p1415, Thomas Nelson Publishers, Nashville

11

[13] *The Collins English Dictionary & Thesaurus*

[14] Michael Molinos, *The Spiritual Guide*, page 6, SeedSowers Christian Books Publishing House PO box 3317 Jacksonville Florida 32206, no publication date

[15] Simon and Garfunkel, *The Sound of Silence*, Columbia Records, released September 1965

[16] David Crowder, *O Praise Him*, from the album, *Remedy*, sixstepsrecords.com 2007

[17] *The Collins English Dictionary & Thesaurus*

12

[18] *http://www.ncbi.nlm.nih.gov/pmc/articles/PMC2077351/* Simon N. Young, Journal of Psychiatry & Neuroscience, November 2007

[19] *Ibid*

13

[20] *Death is nothing at all, author unknown, published by Kevin Mayhew Ltd 2011*

[21] *Charles Henry Brent 1862-1929, What is dying, published by Kevin Mayhew Ltd 2011*

15

[22] *Wikipedia, on grief*
[23] *Expressive Grief, www.expressivegriefcounselling.com*
[24] *The Collins English Dictionary & Thesaurus*
[25] *Elizabeth Kubler-Ross www.ekrfoundation.org*

16

[26] *Mind website www.mind.org.uk*
[27] *Ibid*
[28] *Cited from Mind website www.mind.org.uk*

17

[29] *The Collins Dictionary & Thesaurus*
[30] *Brother Lawrence, Practicing the Presence of God, Eulogy by Joseph de Beaufort, pp34&35, Paraclete Press, Brewster, Massachusetts*
[31] *Ibid, p35*
[32] *Ibid, p38*

18

[33] *The Collins Dictionary & Thesaurus*

20

[34] *Triumph in the Torture Chamber, from the magazine, Heroes of Faith, p29, July-September 2010*

23

[35] *The Twelve Steps a Spiritual Journey, revised edition, p79 RPI publishing, Inc San Diego*
[36] *Attributed to St Augustine, www.goodreads.com*

24

[37] *The Collins Dictionary & Thesaurus*

25

[38] *The Collins Dictionary & Thesaurus*
[39] *Strong's #1515, Spirit Filled Life Bible, p1510, Thomas Nelson Publishers, Nashville*
[40] *Strong's #5432 cited in Spirit Filled Bible, p1907, Thomas Nelson Publishers, Nashville*

BOOKS FOR FURTHER READING

—•◆•—

Mystical Paths to God: Three Journeys: Brother Lawrence's *The Practice of the Presence of God*. St. Teresa of Avila's *Interior Castle*, St. John of the Cross's *Dark Night of the Soul* Wilder Publications, LLC. PO Box3005 Radford VA 24143

Practicing His Presence: Brother Lawrence & Frank Laubach, SeedSowers Christian Books Publishing House PO Box 3317 Jacksonville, Fl 32206

Spiritual Torrents: Jeanne Guyon, SeedSowers PO Box 285 Sargent, GA 30275

Spiritual Guide: Michael Molinos, SeedSowers Christian Books Publishing House, PO Box 3317 Jacksonville, Fl 32206

Battlefield of the Mind: Joyce Meyer, Warner Faith, New York, Boston, Nashville, 1995

Power in Praise: Merlin R. Carothers, Merlin R. Carothers, Dec. 2011, ISBN: 0943026016

Prison to Praise: Merlin R. Carothers, Merlin R. Carothers, Dec. 2011, ISBN: 0943026024